SPRIG
OF
BROOM

SUSAN WHITFIELD

ISBN: 978-0-9968187-0-4 (Trade paperback)
ISBN: 978-0-9968187-1-1 (eBook Edition)
Published in the United States of America

Published by Studebaker Press

Acknowledgements

The novel you hold in your hands would not have been possible without the assistance of others, key among them my first cousin, Beth White May, the genealogist in the family. Through Beth's years of tracing our ancestors, she amassed a treasure of fodder for this author. If only I could live long enough to delve into all of them! Alas, *Sprig of Broom* has been quite a challenge, and I cannot thank you enough, Beth, for all your years of study to make it possible for me to "meet" Geoffrey. I took great leaps of liberty with the historical information, but I hope I did him justice.

Mary Daly, I remember the day my novel "froze" on the screen at 36,000 words. You talked me through the thaw and saved my baby. Then other tech problems arose and you assisted me again and again. I can't thank you enough for always being there for me, not only as technical support but also as my best friend, my navigator on trips, and my assistant at conferences. You are truly a treasure and I love you so much! You are the sister I never had.

Robin Smith, my wonderful editor, thank you so much for squeezing me in with all you had going on especially your move. Thank you for your attention to detail and direction with this challenging novel.

P.M. Terrell, *Sprig of Broom* would not have made it to print without you, my friend. Thank you so much for your generous offering of publishing support.

To numerous historical fiction writers, thank you for advising me on various questions about meshing fact with fiction and when to just let my fictional characters take charge.

Thank you so much, readers of my work. I cannot tell you how much it means for you to ask "When's the next book coming out?" Thank you for your loyal support over several genres.

What can I say about my wonderful and loving family that I have not said in previous acknowledgements? Without love and support from you I might never have finished a book, especially this one, which proved to be my biggest challenge yet. I love you all!

Other Books by Susan Whitfield

The Logan Hunter Mysteries

Genesis Beach

Just North of Luck

Hell Swamp

Sin Creek

Sticking Point

Women's Fiction

Slightly Cracked

Non-Fiction

Killer Recipes

Sprig
of
Broom

Susan Whitfield

Studebaker Press
North Carolina, USA

This book is dedicated to Doyle,
my personal knight in shining armor

In memory of my father, John David Eakins

Descendants of the Knights of the Bath

Whereas in times past upon divers, wise, and honorable considerations it pleased the Royal Predecessors of the Sovereigns of Great Britain and Ireland on occasion of certain august solemnities conferred with great state upon their Royal Issue male, the Princes of the Blood Royal, several at their Nobility, Principal Officers, and other Persons distinguished by their birth, quality, and personal merit that degree of knighthood which hath been denominated the Knighthood of the Bath: and Whereas this association besigning to honour such, wishes it to Be Known That:

Susan Elaine Eakins Whitfield

Being a lineal descendant of a Knight of the Bath is hereby enrolled as member of
Descendants of the Knights of the Bath upon record of:

Sir Geoffrey V Plantagenet

Knighted, invested 1127 during the reign of Henry I

INTRODUCTION

Many years ago I learned from my first cousin, Elizabeth White May, that I was a descendant of a Knight of the Bath. I received a large frame-able certificate and a medal. I proudly displayed both items and have thought for a long time that I might read more about Geoffrey Plantagenet, Count of Anjou, and how he became a knight and married the daughter and heiress of King Henry of England, son of William the Conqueror.

At long last I began to research "Geoffrey the Handsome" and felt compelled to write about his life, giving the best historical account I could, based on my research, along with plenty of fictional twists added for good measure. The section about Geoffrey as a Templar is total fiction and speculation on my part. I imagined since his father helped fund these elite knights, and they had to be nobles and knights to be considered, it was quite possible he was recruited for the Second Crusade.

It is widely reported that Geoffrey liked to wear a sprig of broom blossom in his hat. Broom plant is known as *planta genesta* in Latin, thus, the origin of Geoffrey's surname, Plantagenet. Most historians agree the well-educated Geoffrey had outstanding qualities. He was a warrior through good fortune and his own hard work, dedicating himself to the defense of the community. Honorable to his friends, he was considered more trustworthy than other leaders of his time. He bore malicious offenses from his lady wife—Dowager Empress Matilda—with more patience than most men would, perhaps because she was the king's daughter and heir to the throne of England. Or perhaps he understood her predicament: being female in an age when only men ruled. Whatever the reason, Geoffrey found it pleasant to be away from her for years at a time.

Even though Geoffrey was never a king, he fathered King Henry II and thus began the long reign of Plantagenet kings of England, one of the most iconic dynastic names in medieval European history, providing England with fourteen kings who reigned from 1154-1485.

False face must hide what the false heart doth know
~William Shakespeare

Whitsuntide 1127 A.D.

1

Carts and packhorses trundled behind me, jostled by dusty well-trodden paths from my home in the county of Anjou to my far destination in Rouen in the north of Normandy. I, Count Geoffrey of Anjou, at the age of fifteen summers had been summoned by King Henry of England to marry his daughter, Matilda, many years older and formerly wed. Our marriage would be one of political alliance. Even though my father, Count Fulk of Anjou and the king had once been opposing foes in battle, King Henry arranged the marriage to detach Anjou from a hostile coalition and to assist Matilda—his only living heir—in succeeding him in Normandy and England. I would be knighted, and in so doing strategically place our Norman frontiers under his rule, and further, sire the king's grandchildren. I would be a stranger marrying a stranger with no regard for like-mindedness. Uneasiness flooded me for I was an untested bridegroom.

I was glad for the company of my barons on this arduous journey. Robert of Semblancay came along as my seneschal, keeper of my purse. Hardouin of Saint-Mars I would rely upon for military advice when the future presented conflict

and Robert of Blou for personal protection. Paieri of
Clairville attended horses, set up and dismantled camp each
day, and played a lute as we travelled. Jacquelin of Maille,
the kitchener and my personal if not official jester, kept us
all amused. At times we all joined in a song to pass time or
told jokes to enliven our spirits.

One evening we stopped at a small pond surrounded
by long grass and rested while our mounts grazed with
delight. We decided to set camp early and I plopped down
to watch the sun descend below the grass ahead of us.

After breaking camp early in the morn, my men and I
approached a dip between two knolls and stepped over to
the edge of a shitbrook to let pass a galloping messenger
who seemed oblivious to our presence.

"Godspeed," we shouted in unison.

Back on the well-trodden path, we traveled on with song
and wit from Baron Jacquelin who entertained us from first
light 'til slumber each day.

"Geoffrey, broom is flowering. Shall I fetch you a sprig
for your hat?"

"I would be pleased to have it, Jacquelin." I laughed as
the big man scrambled into the field and pinched off a piece
of bloom. I had grown up with Jacquelin, he a few summers
older, but quite an entertaining fellow with many talents.
He returned and handed me the bloom which I pushed
into the band on my hat.

At last, off in the distance I spied the cathedral, massive
and magnificent and still a good day's foot journey hence.
Even in dawn's light I could see it dwarfed other buildings
around it—even many churches and the castle wall—but
signaled our long tiresome journey neared its end.

An ominous sound unexpectedly penetrated my
thoughts and a cold fog washed over me like damp wool.
My view disappeared as mist eddied and locked me in its
cocoon of eerie dankness, alone. I reached for my blade to

cut through it, hoping to open it up like a boar hog's hide and step out into the light. No opening presented itself. I stopped in my tracks on the rocky road. I knew steep ravines were poised on each side, waiting to beat me to a pulp as I plummeted to the bottom. I could see nothing, but an unworldly and putrid smell invaded my nostrils.

"Blou? Hardouin? Paieri?"

I heard no response from my men, but a low moan grew louder. Did I hear sinister laughter? Could that be possible out here far between two kingdoms? Surely no other fools ventured out at dawn's first light without due cause.

"Jacquelin? Is that your laughter I hear?"

Jacquelin did not respond.

There! Again I heard it. Menacing laughter. I grabbed the hilt of my dagger with determination as an ominous humming sound came closer to me. Could someone . . . or something see me through the fog? I began to shake from dampness or fear of what brought the laughter.

The cackling turned into a low groan and a hag chewing a brown plant appeared just out of my reach, wearing tattered clothes and displaying ragged and rotten teeth, ghastly wild hair, a prunish face, and foul stench.

"Listen and heed," it warned.

More shrill laughter and another voice came from a different direction. I turned in a circle and tried to determine from which way the voice came.

"Mesh becomes chain," a squeaky voice proclaimed behind me.

I blinked, understanding nought. I spun until my lightheadedness dropped me to my knees at the sound of yet another voice.

"Dark of moon brings realm of gloom," a deeper raspier voice disclosed.

"Heat of broom becomes his doom," yet another voice declared. I was surrounded.

"Gloom and doom for man of broom!" This deafening pronouncement came in unison from all the ghastly voices encircling me, making my bones creak.

"Who are you? Show yourselves, old crones," I bellowed, trying not to display fear. But I heard no answer and the fog and the one apparition I could see dissipated. I again had a clear view of the next village, no being of any kind in sight. Where were the barons who had accompanied me from my home land and walked with me only seconds ago?

I turned when I heard a commotion behind me and saw the men running to catch me, Blou in the lead, sword drawn.

"Where did you go, my lord?"

"I have the same question for you, Blou."

"We walked along the road with you until you disappeared into a fog. We nought could find you or hear you. We called out but no answer came."

"You did not hear me call to you?"

"No, my lord."

"Witches surrounded me and separated me from you," I explained.

"For what purpose, my lord?"

"I have no answer, Blou, only riddles that made no sense." I shivered and tried to shake off my disquiet before it gripped me tighter. I gulped in several lungsful of fresh air and gathered my courage before I turned back to the dirt path and adjusted the sprig of broom in my hat that would symbolize the House of Plantagenet. I drew in a breath and looked each man in the eye to assure them of my fearlessness. "Do not be dismayed, men. Let us proceed to Rouen Castle where the King of England and Duke of Normandy awaits our arrival."

"Aye, my lord," the barons responded simultaneously.

Even though I had never met the woman to whom I was espoused and had no feeling of any kind towards her, the prospect of being knighted filled me with compelling emotion. The king had instituted a hierarchy of mailed knights, dedicated to travelling the realm and administering justice. I hoped to do more than merely joust and fulfill my vows within castle walls. My youth cried out for adventure, and on my father's orders I had packed up and proceeded with my companions although not with as much enchantment as they exuded at the prospect of a feast with the king.

"Sing a song of wit, Jacquelin. My nerves unravel me."

"Aye, my lord," Jacquelin replied. Clearing his throat and throwing back his head, he sang a bawdy tune. I quickened my pace, my men steps behind me, and soon felt the heaviness in my chest lessen. The barons boisterously joined Jacquelin in song. All laughed and jostled each other, but none reached out to wallop me. I stopped in the rocky path, motionless for a moment as they quieted behind me.

"Geoffrey?" whispered Hardouin.

"'Tis nought. My innermost thoughts are knotted, although your song, Jacquelin, has lifted my spirit."

"I am pleased, my lord."

"Let us proceed in silence as we approach the king's castle."

The barons looked at each other, shrugged, and followed me. We walked by plowed fields, barns, sheds, and animal pens, clustered near the village and labored by villeins, many of whom lived harsh lives and subsisted on meager vittles. A life I knew little of. Smells of every kind filled my nostrils and rendered me light-headed. Signs of village life greeted us: broken crockery, bones, entrails, human refuge and rotten meat. I held my breath as we passed a large shitbrook, stepped around a man shoveling horse dung into a heap, and picked up our pace once again.

A wooden bridge of great length separated the mud huts and filthy village life from the far more prosperous merchants' houses and shops of stone with thatched roofs. Corn, salted meat, apples, pears and nuts whet my appetite and I slowed to sample a few wares. We made our way around ponies and packhorses through the marketplace and passed hay, dairy products, poultry and fish before a market displayed glass and bed linens in beautiful colors. Farther away I saw the royal castle at Rouen.

We stepped back as priests robed in habits with crucifixes and rosaries hanging from their girdles hurried past us. Curiosity knitted my brow.

"They head to the king's castle, Geoffrey . . . for your ceremony," Hardouin explained.

As we neared the hillock, we stopped once again and gazed upon the moat—the earthwork where stood one of many castles of King Henry—and then crossed the bridge and made our ascent up the steep hill where we were greeted by trumpets announcing my arrival. Crowds gathered and maidens called out to me, "Le Bel." My face flushed with embarrassment as I smiled and walked on, uncomfortable in my own skin. The king's nobles rode out on horseback to greet me and a chevalier handed me reins to ride a handsome steed into the courtyard just ahead. Many more of the king's attendants appeared to welcome us and show us into the Great Hall where we would eat and drink and then be shown our quarters. Marshals led our few pack horses—made skittish by a sudden onslaught of barking dogs—to be stabled.

My heart hitched as the crowd parted and King Henry himself, a bull of a man and the youngest son of William the Conqueror, came to greet me. I dropped to one knee and bowed as he approached.

"Stand," he ordered.

When our eyes met, I was relieved to see a slight smile and a sparkle as he looked up at my tall frame. He embraced my shoulders and kissed my cheek as though I was already a part of his royal family.

"Welcome, Count Geoffrey of Anjou. You are indeed fair and of good stature."

He bade me sit by him on a tufted crimson bench and engaged me in rhetoric about the kingdom's challenges, markedly political.

"As you are aware, your father Fulk and I forged a political alliance to end upheaval and hostility, to bring Normandy under my control as a peaceful state."

"I am aware, Your Grace."

"The Norman castles of Domfront, Exmes and Argentan will form Matilda's dowry."

I nodded, pleased with his announcement and responded as best I could to a multitude of thought-provoking inquiries, although the long journey had tired me. Having been well-schooled even before I knew I would wed King Henry's daughter, the king seemed pleased with my answers. He spoke of his expectations of me, both as a Knight of the Bath and his new son-in-law, before the Night of Vigil began.

"Count Geoffrey, I know you have prepared for knighthood since the age of seven. Your integrity and other worthy assets are well-known throughout the realm. 'Tis quite impressive for one so young. I am markedly impressed with your grammar and rhetoric for such a young age. And what of your counting?"

"I count well, Your Grace."

He smiled and patted my arm. "I am pleased." He clapped his hands and servants appeared with wine and ale for the king, knights and nobles of every station. We moved to a long table board where a banquet of delicacies covered wooden tables for all to enjoy. I caught a glimpse of Jacquelin, who was in his element. He grinned in merriment as he presented tasty morsels from the king's own kitchen.

The palace's paunchy castellan spouted orders with stewards and seneschals keeping count and bottlers and butlers laying a storehouse of wine, beer and water nearby, along with a feast unlike any I had ever witnessed in my young life.

2

After this heartiness of meals, the Hall became solemn, all eyes focused on me again. My knighthood required a religious ceremony with a blessing from the church to go forward and protect it, by use of arms if necessary. Of course my first allegiance was to the king. Before beginning Night of Vigil in the king's chapel, I was led to my ritual bath to purify my body. The bath was hot and filled with rose petals, oil, spices and herbs. I relaxed to such an extent I might have slipped under the water into a deep and eternal sleep if not for the occasional nudge from a king's man to keep me upright. Nevertheless, I felt cleansed, fragrant and calm when the bath was complete.

I dressed in crisp white linen vesture—symbolizing purity—and slipped on a magnificent tunic of gold cloth over which I attached a purple cloak. My hose and silken shoes were black. A sword and shield were placed on the chapel altar as I walked to it and knelt in silent prayer, cloistered, and prodded from time to time by a king's nobleman to keep me awake over the course of ten hours of meditation. Fatigue settled over me, but the king's nobleman did his duty. He left marks on my body when I seemed about to lose consciousness.

By Terce I stirred with relief when doors creaked open and the castellan and chatelaine and staff scurried in. King

Henry and his entourage then entered. Behind them the chapel filled with others to hear mass and a lengthy sermon on the duties of a knight. A sponsor glanced my way and took possession of the sword and shield which were then blessed by a priest and delivered to the king. I knelt again.

"King Henry Beauclerc, King of England and Duke of Normandy, I present to you Geoffrey Plantagenet, Count of Anjou," the sponsor announced.

The king rose from his throne and crossed until he stood before me. Thus began my vows and allegiance to God and to the throne.

"Let us begin Vows and Oath of Knighthood on this tenth day of June in the year of our Lord 1127," King Henry bellowed. Silence filled the huge chapel. "Count Geoffrey Plantagenet, repeat after me: I will stay moral and honorable."

"I will stay moral and honorable," I repeated.

"I will be strong, disciplined, and use my power to protect the weak and defenseless."

"I will be strong, disciplined, and use my power to protect the weak and defenseless," I recited.

"I vow to be loyal, generous, and of noble bearing, to tell the truth, and respect the honor of women."

I echoed the king's words.

"I will guard the honor of fellow knights."

"I will guard the honor of fellow knights."

"I vow to obey my king and to never refuse a challenge from an equal."

"I vow to obey my king and to never refuse a challenge from an equal."

The king continued, "I will fear God and attend His church, keep faith, and persevere to the end in any enterprise begun."

I repeated the final vow with conviction.

King Henry drew the sword, and with the flat of the blade, smote me on the shoulder. "In the name of God, I, Henry Beauclerc, King of England and Duke of Normandy, knight thee, Sir Knight, Sir Geoffrey Plantagenet, Knight of the Order of the Bath. Be brave and loyal all the days of your life."

He placed the sword near my face and I kissed the hilt and took hold of it and the shield, displaying a heraldic standard of six gold lions on a blue background which would represent the House of Plantagenet henceforth. Sponsors attached spurs of gold to my shoes. Whispers reached my ears that no knight had ever before been so elaborately adorned.

As I stood, music and fanfare filled the chapel and spilled into the courtyard beyond. I leapt upon my mighty steed to show off my riding skills, waving my sword and lance as the crowd shouted. The celebration feast commenced with my fellow knights, nobles, and royalty, including the barons who had accompanied me on my journey. Minstrels and troubadours provided entertainment and the festivities became rowdy.

"I see her, my lord," Blou whispered in my ear after I alit from my horse.

"Where?" I turned to see a breathtaking woman staring at me from the other side of the courtyard, her ladies-in-waiting whispering and giggling behind her. To my surprise my betrothed stuck her nose into the air, swished her gown around, and vanished. Little did I know at the time that her actions were a portent.

Blou poked me. "The beautiful lady seems not so impressed with you, Geoffrey. Do you think you can master all *that*, my friend?" He laughed. "Let me know if you need assistance." He clutched his crotch and adjusted his codpiece to its best advantage before he disappeared into the crowd and left me with a fiery face, my fist clenched and strong words on my lips.

Blou and I had been friends since early childhood and I knew much of him. As a bastard, he was raised by a mean earl. Blou learned to defend himself against the man with many weapons, and rumors abounded that he himself had killed the earl and disposed of his body where no man could ever find it. I had never asked. He now preferred staying in the shadows, often as a hired mercenary. He had been enlisted by my father on occasion, his assignments never discussed in my presence.

Blou was much older than me and owned an arrogant swagger even though he had a brooding nature. I had heard he bedded many a fair maiden and oft times another man's lady wife. Even though he had been loyal to me thus far, I kept both eyes on him. He oft times flirted with dangers I shunned. He could teach me plenty, but I had no desire to learn much of it.

Fanfare continued as my men and I proceeded to horses drawn up and distributed for us. A bedecked Spanish steed the color of midnight stopped in front of me. I was fitted with a cuirass—a fitted double layered mail breastplate and back plate—which no lance or javelin could pierce. Iron boots covered my feet and gold spurs were bound to them. A helmet covered in gems protected my head. I was presented with a Weyland sword from the royal treasury.

Armed to the hilt, I rode the handsome steed throughout the countryside, my stout horse fleet, poised and graceful in his speed. I had never had such a horse. I named him Honor. Once Honor and I were accustomed to one another, the rest of the day was devoted to military games.

Celebration of my knighthood lasted for a sinnight. I took opportunities given me to knock Blou from his mount to send a convincing message his way. A number of times I throttled him as he passed me, wrenching his arm the last time. I respected his reputation as a soldier, but he would learn to respect my position and my prowess or endure consequences.

"What is amiss, Geoffrey?"

"You honor me not."

Blou's face reddened with pain or mayhap anger. "I *do*, my lord. Truly."

"Then *show* it. Regard the title I hold. Respect our friendship from childhood. I will take nothing less," I hissed at him from atop my mount.

He jerked his head back in surprise at my action, a look of menace flashing across his face. "You would threaten me, knowing my reputation as a mercenary?" He stepped in my direction.

"I respect your accomplishments, Blou. I want the same from you." I maneuvered my mount and trotted away from him.

I dismounted when a bell signaled the end of games with yet another feast ahead. As I headed towards the hall, Blou ran up beside me.

"Sir Geoffrey, I make an apology for my earlier remark. 'Twas out of place. I beg your forgiveness. It will happen no more."

I looked over at his sincere countenance. "You are forgiven, Blou, but I hold you to your promise."

"Forever, my lord." He bowed and stepped back to display the respect I had won. I needed to trust Blou. I wished not to make an enemy of him. I had made my point.

My next glimpse of Jacquelin came in a flurry of food, drink and condiments set before us after jousting that rainy day. Game birds had been roasted and adorned with colorful feathers; hare and deer had been plated, and swans and pigs followed. Meadow herbs and spices of ginger, clove, and cinnamon from the Far East delighted my tongue. Pastries and sweetmeats appeared along with omelets, breads, berries, vegetables, and fish—carp, salmon, sturgeon and roasted oysters. I had never dined on such exotic cuisine and ate until the excess sickened me. In all that time I saw not Matilda, who was, no doubt, preparing for marriage.

The following morning after we broke our fasts in separate quarters, King Henry and his queen, Lady Matilda, and their attendants, my barons and I set out on a long journey to LeMans, where I would again see my father and step-mother and where the nuptial sacrament would be performed by archbishops, bishops, abbots and priests. As we departed, we rode through muck, the king and his entourage avoiding the worst parts of common life by taking to hills reserved solely for royal use.

Anticipation enveloped me as I moved along with the rest of the company, not noticing our surroundings much until again small alleys and huts became grander cleaner streets leading to handsome houses kept in good repair. My eyes locked on a gatehouse with a crenellated tower indicating the owner's great wealth.

"Malcolm, a revered financier, lives there," Semblancay pointed out to me.

"But *you* are my financier." I must have looked alarmed.

"At the moment, mayhap, but he is there if you ever need him."

I nodded, somewhat relieved he indicated no plan to abandon me right away. We walked on, occasionally stepping to the edge of the path to relieve ourselves. We came at last to a castle, stone fortresses making up the keep, a round tower and a gatehouse.

Just beyond the castle I spied the awe-inspiring cathedral where the marriage ceremony would take place. People scurried like worker bees decorating a spectacular hive for their queen. I paused to take in the grandeur of LeMans Cathedrale, the most majestic structure I had ever seen. It dwarfed all around it, even the tallest of trees. Gothic spires were bedecked with banners representing nobility from near and far. Intricate details abounded and I kept my eyes on my destination as my barons and I rode onward. The road took use through throngs of enthusiastic well-wishers with horse carts, some of the boisterous crowd jostling us around when the road narrowed in dangerous places or mud waited to ruin fine apparel. As we neared, I stopped again to study immense stained-glass windows, each one taller than my five men and I standing on each other's shoulders.

"Come, Sir Geoffrey," Blou whispered. "You are expected inside the castle of LeMans, my lord."

I caught up with the royal entourage and rode Honor into the castle where I welcomed a good night's slumber.

❖ ❖ ❖

Even though I slept well, the wedding day began with an abrupt jostle to wake me and get me moving towards the cathedral in all my finery. Jacquelin concocted a breakfast feast for me and my barons, including himself. Afterwards my men dressed me in royal knight attire without headgear and we proceeded to the cathedral, where bells broadcast the coming event. I understood Matilda prepared for the lavish ceremony, having been escorted to Rouen by her half-brother, Earl Robert of Gloucester, and a trusted friend, Earl Brien fitzCount. I heard whispers that she wished not to marry me and consented after the Archbishop of Tours intervened and convinced her to fulfill the king's wishes. Her reluctance added to my own apprehension.

LeMans Cathedrale lit with a thousand torches was magnificent, filled with mahogany, stone and glass and all due pomp expected of a royal wedding. I stopped to sign a pedestal scroll just inside the entrance, knelt briefly, and then walked the length of the cathedral. An elderly cleric was escorted to the right choir loft as music began to play. I presumed this to be the Archbishop Lanfranc, a personal friend of the king.

Robed monks entered and walked to the choir loft, chanting as they moved. Bishops and archbishops dressed in ceremonial garments made their way down the long aisle with their standards of office presented before them. They stood in an impressive line opposite the choir. Another bishop entered from a side room and sat on the left choir side. The vicar who would officiate took his place near the high altar in the center, behind which was displayed the blue and gold House of Plantagenet standard. A door opened near the back of the cathedral where my father, Fulk V and my step-mother, Melisende, emerged and moved down the aisle, bobbed their heads in my direction, and seated themselves on the right front pew.

The vicar gestured for a chancellor to escort me behind a door on the right until the cathedral filled to capacity with invited royal guests and dignitaries from all the realm. My barons were nowhere to be found. I felt relief when my father entered the room and embraced me.

"Good fortune smiles on you, my son," he said, "as does it shine on me. As you know, my marriage to the beautiful Melisende bids me on a long journey to the Holy Land. She is the established heir of Jerusalem, the capital of Israel. I, as king, promised to defend the Holy City from the Muslim champion, Zengi."

"I heard the good news, Father."

"Ah, I am King of Jerusalem. I undertake all future responsibilities there knowing the county of Anjou is in your good hands. Geoffrey, some will not be pleased at the change of command but you prove yourself strong, intelligent, and a worthy warrior. I trust lords and nobles will welcome you."

I nodded and a smile spread across my face. I now controlled Anjou in my own right and had been knighted. In moments I would marry the heir to the throne of England.

My father left to sit with his new wife and I remained alone reverently listening to soft music and the movements on the other side of the door as the cathedral filled and awaited the entrance of the royal family and the king's daughter, Matilda. When summoned, I stepped out just in time to kneel as King Henry and Queen Adeliza walked down the aisle—she a few steps behind—both dressed in exquisite royal attire. Once they were seated in left pews near the altar, music bellowed from organ pipes and I stared at palatial stained-glass windows with my back to my bride as she progressed down the long aisle with no attendants. Her father met her beside me. After the vicar gave a blessing, my future father-in-law began his formal statement.

"I, Henry Beauclerc, King of England and Duke of Normandy, give Empress Matilda Maud Alice, my daughter, in betrothal to Sir Geoffrey V Plantagenet, Knight of the Order of the Bath and Count of Anjou, son of Fulk V, King of Jerusalem here and forever more."

My father stepped forward and declared, "I Fulk V, King of Jerusalem, give my eldest son, Sir Geoffrey V Plantagenet, Knight of the Order of the Bath and Count of Anjou, to the king's daughter, Empress Matilda Maud Alice, with the understanding that he maintain strength and vigilance as her guardian, here and forever more."

Henry then stated, "My daughter Matilda will abide by him with the virtue of a lady. She will cling to him in constancy and together they will bear heirs to the throne of England."

Matilda made a noise—a sigh. Or was it a hiss? I glanced her way but her face was unreadable. King Henry cleared his throat and looked at his daughter with a scowl on his face before stepping back.

Matilda and I promised our faithfulness one to the other and looked straight ahead as solemn masses conducted by archbishops, bishops, abbots, and priests of all ranks blessed our union. She lightly touched my outstretched wrist, as was customary. I stole a few glances at my betrothed throughout the ceremony that joined us and merged our lands. Matilda's gown made of burnished silk resembled armor and fitted well enough to show her tiny waist and hips and ample breasts, demurely covered. A hint of strong shoulder peeked between the strapless gown and the attached cloak pooling around her feet. The bodice was embroidered in the same thread, a silk belt tied at her hips. A delicate wreath of jewels adorned her dark hair. Matilda was stunning, but as beautiful as she was, she was rigid in stature and feeling. No smile dared show itself on her countenance.

Once the ceremony was complete, I took her hand in mine and led her into the Great Hall and over to a high balcony where we waved to crowds below while a cacophony of bells rang to announce our marriage. When we stepped back into the Great Hall a magnificent feast began, and a rare tiered white flour wedding cake awaited us. White frosting was covered with flowers of spun sugar that had the mark of Jacquelin. I had seen him practicing back in Anjou even before we knew I would become a knight in England.

"Slice a piece and feed it to your bride," my father whispered in my ear.

I pulled my Weyland sword and sliced the cake, carefully pulled it from the rest, and laid it gently on a pewter plate. I handed my sword off and offered the plate to my bride.

"You are to pick it up and put it to my lips," she said through clenched teeth.

I did as instructed, somewhat embarrassed that I knew not of this ritual of marriage.

I fed her a morsel and she chewed and swallowed with delight. She then fed me a morsel.

Weariness and uncertainty crept into my thoughts, but throngs of attendees rejoiced, danced, and made merry with wandering minstrels, acrobats, jugglers, and clowns throughout three sinnights. When the celebration wound down, all those who had attended the wedding ceremony departed with a gift from the royal family.

King Henry left me alone with his daughter, my new lady wife, giving us each a kiss of peace as he left on his journey back to Rouen and from there on to England. Matilda traveled with me, accompanied by my father and step-mother, to more lavish ceremony at Angers, the capital of Anjou. Churches were decorated and clergy held candles, books and crosses, and sang hymns of praise upon our arrival.

I stopped at a crag and looked ahead at the castles of Loches high on the topmost hill above the town street, at Monthazan across the river on another hill, and at Langeais, just inside the wall, all decorated with festivity. Bells rang out to signal our approach. Monthazan would accommodate Matilda and me now and when we visited on future journeys as Count and Countess of Anjou we had access to all three.

Anjou, known as "the garden of Normandy," displayed magnificently plush land kept fertile by the river Maine which flowed between two hills of rolling vineyards upon which the town was built. Woods and valleys were lush perfection. Pride rose in me as Matilda and I later walked alone by the riverbank on the grounds at Monthazan without fear of being followed or mobbed. Neither of us spoke a word, but I studied her confusing disposition as we moved along. When dark clouds appeared over mountain tops, I reached for her hand.

"We must hasten. A storm approaches." She took my hand and I led her around rocky paths towards our castle as wind whipped her skirts about. We stepped through the threshold just as the leading cloud emptied itself. Gaiety had filled the streets below until the rain dampened all who remained outdoors, and streets and paths emptied.

During the past sinnights my lady wife and I had been in close proximity but a chill overtook me every time Matilda's eyes met mine. Now observable awkwardness lay heavy between us in the bedchamber. I took great care in preparing for my wedding's consummation by wiping my teeth with a cloth. I swilled white wine and chewed parsley to sweeten my breath. I eyed the bed itself, raised not on one but two platforms centered between stone walls. Heavy tapestry drapes—tied at each corner of the bed—awaited a snatch to provide privacy under the bed's fabric canopy. Matilda had disappeared to remove her wet clothing with the aid of her lady-in-waiting.

As we later approached the marriage bed after her return, she huffed at me. "Geoffrey, my husband, I promised my father a male heir to the throne. We must procreate, but I take no pleasure in it with a mere *boy* who is no more than a *count*," she announced with great emphasis. She walked over to the platform and stomped up to the bed, turned back towards me, rucking up her wedding gown skirts to grant me access. I stared at her nakedness but remained motionless.

"Well?" Her tone—a guttural growl—and its accompanying demeanor unnerved me. "I am now your lady wife. Take me!"

"'Tis not as I anticipated," I stuttered nervously, my groin not responding to her in a pleasant manner.

I walked over to her and pushed her back on the bed, wrestling her skirts aside and over her head. After removing my belt and dropping my braies, I struggled to enter her roughly, but she neither flinched nor made noises other than a few groans. 'Twas over in a matter of minutes and I moved away from her again, a feeling of disgust at myself in taking her in such manner.

She sat upright, adjusted her bodice and rearranged the attire she had no interest in removing in my presence.

"Humph, I hardly felt a thing." Her eyes sparkled with meanness and animosity, her voice as sour as unripe persimmon as she stared at me.

Anger fumed within me. I wanted to spit out foul words at the king's daughter—now my lady wife—but instead I dressed and left the bedchamber. The breath-taking experience I had heard so much about was not what I had expected at all. Very disappointing, indeed. I knew an heir must be achieved so there would be many more opportunities to bed my lady wife, but I had little eagerness to do so. With mixed and troubling emotions, I walked Monthazan's dank and dark halls until the storm broke. With a distant crack of thunder as my invitation, I stepped outside and followed the Maine River around the property and away from Matilda. I hoped I could calm my anger before I had to face her again. I skipped rocks and heaved a heavy boulder into the river to release my tension.

✤ ✤ ✤

The woman I had married was not hospitable in the least and nights became a time of dread and irritation. Each time we came together in our marriage bed, my lady wife remained rigid in my embrace until I let her go and moved away.

"I refuse to coerce you longer," I said in anger a few nights later.

Her expression softened a bit. "I will try to make our marriage work, Geoffrey, for the sake of my father and the kingdom's need for future heirs. But I have no tender feelings for you and I cannot force them."

"An unfortunate predicament we share, my lady wife,"
I responded honestly and with a bite in my tone.

She appeared shocked at my outburst but I know not
why my remark surprised her. She had spoken to me in
overtones of malice since first we met. She had snarled,
hissed and growled at me. How could I perform under such
vexing circumstances? Rage gushed through my body and I
pounded pillows and coverlets, watching her cower. I
snatched pillows from behind her, making her wince. Would
I strike her? No. But restraint I found difficult.

After another fitful night that should have been joyous,
I rose early in a foul mood and proceeded down a long
corridor at Loches Castle in search of a friendly face. Alas,
my father and his entourage were gone. I remembered the
hag's words: "Mesh becomes chain." Having been knighted,
I now felt chained to a mean-spirited woman for whom I
had no affection. Had this been the crone's meaning?

3

During the following days spent on our journey to King Henry at Westminster Palace in Anglo-Norman England, few words were exchanged between my lady wife and me. My barons accompanied us at a slight distance—seeming to sense the hostility between us—and entertained themselves with song on occasion. I longed to be one of them, single with no allegiance other than to the king. Once we boarded the long ship, my lady wife walked to a gap in the prow where she remained with arms folded over her breasts, and staring out across the channel. She had nought to say until the dankness of salty air took our breaths away and waves became so rough she held on to me to eject the last food of which she had partaken. Once she stabilized, she again took up the posture of a discontented bride, her nose held as high as she could lift it in scorn. A keen of gulls followed in our wake, their squeak causing me further annoyance. We landed well on English soil and completed the rest of our journey with no regard for one another.

❖ ❖ ❖

"The king summons you," proclaimed a sergeant-at-arms not long after our arrival.

I blew out my breath with force and finished dressing in clean attire.

"*Now*, Sir Geoffrey," the king's servant emphasized. "No one keeps the king waiting."

I glared at him in passing and headed towards the king's private chamber, the door open from the inside by the king's chamberlain as I approached. After entering, I knelt, then walked half-way to him and knelt again.

"Godspeed, sire."

"Geoffrey!" bellowed my royal father-in-law. He looked about him and with a wave of his arm dismissed his chamberlain and Locksley, the groom of the stool, who closed the door behind him.

"My daughter cries. She is not pleased with you. *I* am not pleased. Discontentment rules the palace. You are to keep her content. Did I not make myself clear when first we met?"

"You did, Your Grace."

"Well? What do you have to say for yourself?"

"My performance has been disappointing, sire. She squawks and I shrivel." My cheeks warmed with embarrassment at my own words, spoken aloud to the father of my lady wife. I hung my head. "I have no experience in these matters." My voice broke and I flushed since being unmanned by my lady wife seemed not humiliating enough.

"Ah." The king nodded. "I am certain you have sufficient virility, Geoffrey, but you lack experience. That is an easy fix. You must enter instruction. I want you to practice, practice, practice!"

"But, sire, Matilda befuddles me. I can find no love, no connection between us."

"My boy, come here and sit." He patted to his huge plush ottoman and I lowered myself before the king's knees. "Turbulence comes to all marriages. I know my daughter to be antagonistic at times, 'tis true." He shook his head again.

"She was wed to the Emperor of Germany who died. She was young. As an empress, Matilda absorbed a deep sense of her regality and an understanding that ruthlessness and reconciliation could both be vital weapons in a ruler's armory. As regent, she made decisions for the country in the emperor's absence and with his blessing for many seasons." The king sighed deeply. "Women and power make an uneasy alliance, my son-in-law. She returned to me a young woman with an imperial title and a high degree of haughtiness.

At times she is an intolerable shrew!" he yelled out. "She clings to an air of authority which is unbecoming, but her heart hurts, Geoffrey," the king added in a softer voice. "She was merely eight summers when she became queen and married at twelve years to become an empress. Do not judge her with extreme harshness. Matilda needs your kindness, your gentle spirit, until you become more familiar with each other. She grew up in utmost splendor, you see. She was one of the most important women in Europe. She still prefers to be called empress. Doing so might help your cause."

I had no plan to call my lady wife an empress. She was now a countess and nothing more.

"I understand, but I know not how to per . . . proceed, Your Grace."

"Are you saying you have *never* been tested, lad?"

I shook my head with embarrassment.

"I see now that I have, indeed, plucked but a green bud from a tender vine, but never fear, for a remedy is in great supply." He smiled down at me.

I nodded at the king, relieved to know he had an answer for the problem.

He continued, "Courtesans will stand in line to teach you the fine art of love-making, Geoffrey the Handsome. Lessons will at first be exhausting but pleasurable nonetheless."

Speech abandoned me. I had a fortnight ago pledged faithfulness to my lady wife, his own daughter.

"Do you have nothing to say?" He leaned down towards me, his eyes trained on me.

"Your Grace, I am but a lad wedded to a most beautiful woman who has known true love. I seem to fail at every turn. Matilda only shows loathing and indifference for me and an aloofness I cannot subdue. No lessons will change that, I wager."

"My young lad, you have much to learn about being a man," the king whispered near me. "Pump yourself," the king blurted out, leaning towards me with a wink of his eye.

I blinked at him in shock. "Sire?"

"Take matters into your own hands. My boy, must I instruct you on *that*?" He and I stared at one another for a brief moment before he turned and called out to his chamberlain. "The boy is as green as fresh moss." The chamberlain glanced at me but said nought.

"About your wager, Geoffrey. You would lose. You will begin lessons at once. I will speak to my daughter about accepting her responsibilities to me, to this kingdom and to her husband." He turned his head and called out again.

"Farfour!"

"Sire?" The sergeant-at-arms head popped through heavy drapes. He had without doubt bent an ear to our delicate conversation.

"Lead Sir Geoffrey Plantagenet to the chapel for meditation and counsel."

Farfour blinked. "At once!"

"As you wish, sire."

"And Farfour, make discreet inquiries to align Sir Geoffrey with a practiced courtesan who can teach him intimate secrets of passion, and report to me."

"Aye, sire."

Farfour bowed and led me out, my face flushing with embarrassment.

4

After meaningless meditation, I decided I would take the opportunity to present further grievances to the king. As I neared his chamber, I saw Matilda enter, so I slipped into a curtained alcove right outside the wooden doors to wait for her departure.

I could hear their conversation from my position. I had not meant to over-hear, but I found moving now would get me caught and accused anyway. So I stilled myself and listened.

"You sent for me, Father?"

The king's voice was far from pleasant. "I have sent your husband for training in matters that concern you, but you must subject yourself to Geoffrey's authority, Matilda. Resist him *not*. I expect heirs," Henry uttered. "You owe a marital debt, noblesse oblige!"

"I know, Father, but—"

"No buts will be tolerated, Matilda!" His bellow echoed. "I will hear no more of your taunting that boy."

"And he *is* that," she spoke in an ugly tone of voice.

"Geoffrey is quite capable of managing this situation with a little experience and encouragement, but no man can perform under duress and antagonism." The king's tone softened. "You must cuddle him, encourage him, fondle him."

"I know how to do it, Father! I don't need your commentary on conjugal duties."

"And that tone you take must end! Respect this crown or you will suffer the consequences, Matilda."

Silence made me hold my own breath.

Then the king continued. "Imbibe if you must do so, but be gentle and pleasant to your husband, Sir Geoffrey Plantagenet."

I heard Matilda scoff.

"Hear this, my daughter: if marriage vows are not *fully* consummated in private, then there will be public consummation!"

"Father, no!"

"Leave me, Matilda, and think on these things. I have spoken."

I felt a smile of satisfaction spread over my face but stayed hidden until my lady wife's arrogant footsteps faded away at the other end of the long hall. I had no further need to bother King Henry—of whom I was growing fonder—so I walked the same long hall to where I found Farfour as I turned the corner.

"Sir Geoffrey, I have been searching for you. You are to go to the blue bedchamber at the right rear of the castle," he whispered.

"For what purpose?"

"The king orders it, my lord," Farfour said emphatically. "Anon."

Meditation had done little to calm my nerves but I gathered myself and headed down another lengthy corridor, my boots leaving an echo as I walked, irritated I spent exceeding more time inside castle walls than outside on horseback. Entering the unfamiliar chamber, I closed the heavy door behind me. I had never been in this room far from the main chambers. The bed was not massive but had netting overhead and silk curtains on which were painted human genitals in all positions imaginable. A table beside it held an array of items I could not identify.

As I studied the bed and table, I sensed I was not alone in the room and turned to see a slight girl not much older than myself dressed in gossamer that left nothing to my imagination. She spoke not a word but looked me over with curiosity, appraising my worth, no doubt. Her ginger hair spilled down her back and over her shoulders to hide just a bit of her white breasts.

The heavy door opened and the royal sergeant-at-arms appeared.

"You will be cloistered together in this bed chamber until some physical activity takes place in which you are both a party." With that announcement, he closed the door and we heard metal lock the door from the outside.

My stomach lurched.

The girl moved towards me with caution.

"My lord?"

"I …" I gulped in air. "What beauty is this before me? Does my imagination run mad?"

"Touch and you shall see that I am real."

"I dare not."

"You are a Knight of the Bath. You can dare anything." She smiled seductively. "I am here to help you, my lord." She replied in a sweet whisper while letting the gossamer chemise fall from her shoulders to the floor beneath her feet and stepping out of it to display her physical beauty. She came to me as I stood a statue in a stupor. I made a feeble attempt to guard my space. She reached out and touched my clothed chest and I flinched.

"You are a tall one," she whispered.

I managed a nod. "Your . . . name?" My voice trembled along with the rest of me.

"I am Annique, summoned to teach you matters of passion." She stepped closer and nudged me towards the bed's foot bench where I plopped, somewhat shocked at her boldness.

"You're so young."

"No younger than you, my lord," she whispered in my ear. She licked it and sucked my earlobe into her mouth, nibbling on it as though it were a morsel of fresh pork belly. I was held hostage with no complaint. My member jumped in my braies and parts of me I had never met began to tingle. My heart rammed itself into my throat and choked me, pulsing there. My eyes darted around the room, not sure if they should feast upon the magnificent creature who enticed me.

"You tremble. Try to relax." She removed my under tunic and massaged my back and shoulders and then my chest, rubbing and pulling my nipples until they ached.

My eyes came to rest on her angelic face and I allowed myself to relax as she smiled and touched my skin, my body succumbing to her unrelenting seduction. My heart pounded as blood rushed into parts of my body I knew not well, giving me a sensation like no other.

"You are allowed to touch me, my lord." She placed my hand on one of her breast buds and her body and mine became more alive.

She untied my braies and massaged me in a manner I was not accustomed to, our breathing rapid and ragged.

Unable to speak, I allowed myself to enjoy the euphoric pleasure the girl heaped upon me, becoming a victim of passion.

A victim? Hardly.

As her hands clamped both sides of my chest, she lowered her head and touched her lips to my member, now jumping with excitement even as I sat rigid and tried to hide all emotion.

"Do this to yourself." She took my hand and held it there, working me into a pleasure I had never experienced, my body throbbing until I exploded. She wiped away drip and rose to smile at me.

"You did well. Continue to do that until you feel confident. I must go now."

"Where?"

She bowed her head. "I have others awaiting my visit this day. I will see you here tomorrow after Vespers." She slipped the gossamer over her head and disappeared behind thick velvet curtains.

I sat, taking in all that had happened, a brief but enjoyable encounter, indeed. Once dressed, I banged on the door. When I heard the latch unlock, I made no eye contact with the sergeant-at-arms but cleared my throat and walked away in haste.

✥ ✥ ✥

Private tutorials in the fine art of lovemaking continued on a daily basis, and with each encounter Annique taught me more, my personal discontentment with Matilda suppressed in the presence of this lovely and passionate woman. In between visits a thick layer of wanting absorbed me. After a fortnight passed and I had proven myself a worthy lover according to the courtesan, I left the blue chamber feeling more relaxed and confident in my ability.

"Geoffrey?"

I stiffened at my lady wife's voice behind me and turned to see her at the other end of the hall, walking in my direction with convicting eyes set upon me.

"Matilda?"

"My husband," she said as she came to face me, "come to my bedchamber tonight."

"For what purpose?"

"Oh, Geoffrey, my dear husband," she whispered in a

sweet yet sarcastic tone, "you know why. We must create an heir for my father, the King of England."

I gulped in air, not sure I was ready to show my new skills to my lady wife or if I could perform in her condescending presence.

"I ... I know not that I am ready to bed you, Matilda."

She gave my upper arm a slight nudge. "Men are eternally ready. I am certain it will be fine. How hard can it be?" With that comment she laughed and walked past me.

Indeed. Or how limp?

❖ ❖ ❖

I knocked on Matilda's door late, after watching her drink an abominable amount of wine at the evening meal. I had no drink. I needed to be alert for this latest unnerving encounter with my lady wife. Unhappy duty overcame dread.

Matilda was in the bed with a linen coverlet pulled up to her bare shoulders to indicate that she wore nothing at all. Wine made her naughty and amicable and I quickly found myself aroused. Using the knowledge Annique taught me, I made love to my lady wife for the first time. She seemed satisfied and I felt confident I had performed well. Mayhap now Matilda and I could relax and fulfill our duty to the king.

❖ ❖ ❖

I continued lessons with Annique and learned even more about a woman's body and my own in the process. Daylight was filled with coupling with Annique and nights with an inebriated but more cordial Matilda. As much as I missed jousting and tournaments, they became a distant memory when my tutor drew near.

"You shiver," Annique whispered after touching my bare skin.

"This castle has no warmth," I said. She studied me, her eyes drawing me in.

"I will warm you," Annique whispered with a smile. I fell into her arms and we spent the remainder of day's light entwined.

At the gloaming, Annique dressed, wearing a forlorn look.

"Sir Geoffrey, I will see you no more."

"What mean you?" I sat up and stared at her, disregarding my nakedness.

"You no longer need me."

"But I *do*, Annique. I—"

"Shhhh, say nothing. I have taught you well, Sir Geoffrey the Handsome. You need me no longer." Her eyes reddened but her voice quaked not.

"But I *want* you," I stated in all honesty. I hopped from the bed covers to hold her.

"You must take what you have learned and pleasure your lady wife. Give the king heirs. 'Tis your duty."

"But when can I—" I reached for her but she stepped back.

"It ends here," she whispered, touching my lips with her gentle fingertips, fingertips I had grown to love having all over my body. Fingertips that had aroused my manhood and taught me much about my body and myself. Before I could sweep her into my arms, the slight beauty slid behind a curtain and disappeared. I ripped and tore at drapes, thrashing them about in anger and frustration, but Annique was gone. My heart felt heaviness like none I had ever known.

5

Daily jousting and warlike games of hunting amused me and kept me occupied, away from Matilda and my tempting thoughts of Annique. Some nights were spent besting fellow knights at chess or checkers. I welcomed distance and time spent with other knights outside the dark cold castle walls when time allowed. I lost myself in preparing strategies to outwit the older and more experienced knights. One of my war horses, Warrior—the color of a cloud whitened by sun—was powerful and easily held me even in full armor.

Fights and tournaments became a routine for all knights not on a mission for the king, with I the youngest, clad in armor and a steel helmet for protection. My lance, long stout spear, sword, and battle ax added to the weight my steed must carry.

For a while our tournaments were play wars, but I knew I was preparing for conflicts against other kingdoms and perhaps in foreign lands. Sometimes galleries were erected so the king himself could attend. Noblemen and ladies filled the arena to watch two champions mount strong war horses and take a stand at opposite ends of the list. Heralds blasted trumpets and mailed knights spurred and met with a clash of shield and spear, trying to unhorse one another.

Not all jousting was in full harness. From the age of seven, I had participated in tournaments, first to score points for body hits, breaking another's lance and the most points for knocking an opponent from his horse, all of us dressed in chain mail. I progressed to more dangerous jousts where two opponents squared off on opposite sides and ends of a fence and one or both had injuries by the end of the event. Now each level of combat taught me war strategies, and I became more confident in my role as a knight than in my role as a husband.

The fact that I could fight equally well with both hands gave me a great advantage over other knights on the field, even Hardouin and Blou. Warrior carried me well, and when I jumped to the ground, I used my sword to circle, feint, thrust, parry and riposte with either hand. I practiced gymnastics in varying degrees of dress so I could do somersaults in armor if it became necessary to avoid injury. My body became a force all its own.

Today's joust—on an intense level—could end in death, but my pent-up anger and frustration with Matilda made me a fierce competitor, riding on to a field, attacking all I encountered with no fear of bloodshed or my own death. My full metal and helmet protected me as I knocked men to the ground with great power, hearing them call me heartless.

Perhaps I am heartless.

Motivated by my father's promise to attach me to the Knights Templar some time in the future, I fought not in play but with a ferociousness that emerged from deep within, often inflicting serious injury on those who competed against me. Hardouin and Blou practiced military maneuvers in the countryside for the most part, preparing to join me in a joust or a real battle at an appointed time. Hardouin, the elder of the two, had years of military knowledge and Blou was known as one of the best mercenaries a knight could acquire, although his secret feats were not open to discussion. Both men hoped to elevate their status from soldier to knight by valor on the battlefield.

Hardouin and I did combat. He dealt hard blows, but I outmaneuvered him and surprised him with my other hand.

"You must remember that age has slowed me, but I can still best you in military strategy in the field," Hardouin said as I helped him up. "Keep in mind that you will encounter men as young and as powerful as you, Sir Geoffrey."

I nodded in the knowledge that he was right as he limped away.

"Sir Geoffrey?"

I turned to see Paieri walking towards me, holding reins of horses in one hand and a squiggly pile of muck with the other.

"What have you here, Paieri?"

"I found this rag of a lad at the dung heap, my lord."

I held my nose and looked the rag over, took a piece of clean cloth and wiped the face to reveal two large brown eyes and trembling lips. "What name are you?"

The boy spit mud or dung at the ground. "Leofrick, m'lord. Frick."

"Can you find no better place than the dung heap to wallow?"

"I was thrown there by wicked men who no longer wanted me to accompany them, m'lord."

"Family?"

"No, m'lord. I have no family. They burned to ashes in the hut we called home. These vicious men picked me up along the roadside and fed me. They were at first cordial but rapidly their true selves emerged. I became a slave to them, m'lord."

"I see." I looked at the boy's blinking eyes and turned to Paieri. "Take the horses to stable and this boy along with you. Mayhap the trough will make him more fragrant."

"Aye, my lord. I can find him a clean garment as well and mayhap a morsel of bread."

The boy smiled, bowed, and followed Paieri.

Blou then advanced at a quick pace. "Sir Geoffrey, we have been summoned by the king. I am to find Hardouin as well. We are to make haste."

A sudden anxiousness overtook me. "I will meet you there."

When Blou and Hardouin joined me at the end of the long corridor, we walked on together, huge doors opening as we approached. My barons slowed their pace, allowing me to enter first and bow as they took a knee behind me.

"Your Grace," we said in unison.

Henry gestured me forward. "Come forth at once, Sir Geoffrey Plantagenet." The king seldom addressed me with full honor, thus I knew I had been summoned on official business of high royal order. "Your father beckons us to send a force to Anjou where discontent has brought an uprising. As you know, Fulk resides now in Jerusalem and the county of Anjou is left unmanned. I instituted a system of representatives dedicated to travelling the countryside, and to other countries if necessary, to administer justice and fairness. I am sending you and this small circle of men to squelch this uprising in Normandy. You are, after all, Count of Anjou. Attend to this matter with expedience and return to carry out your duties to your king." The king owned a vexed demeanor. "There is still discontent in this castle, Sir Geoffrey."

"Always, sire." I felt a flush on my face and glanced towards my barons who looked confused. "When should we depart?"

"A message was sent to the marshal to ready your steeds. You leave at once. Godspeed!"

We bowed and walked to the door. Once in the hall, we smiled.

"Your time has come to do real battle, Sir Geoffrey. Let us about it then," Hardouin said. "I will devise a plan as we ride."

"What was the king's meaning about discontent here, my lord?" Blou looked in my direction. "Have we not settled our disagreement?"

"I know not his meaning," I lied and clenched my jaw, "but I am quite certain it has nought to do with you." To change the subject, I elbowed him. "Mayhap this uprising will deliver long overdue knighthood to each of you."

They grinned and punched each other likewise.

My chest pounded with excitement as we picked up our pace and headed to the stables where Paieri had horses ready—Warrior and Honor for me—along with packs on mules loaded with supplies to sustain us on our journey.

"Paieri, you have prepared as though we leave 'til summer next," I said.

"'Tis best to have excess rather than less than needed, Sir Geoffrey. And this is the time to test Honor and Warrior. I have new bows from the bowyer and all the arrows the fletcher had in store. Each horse has been checked and I am confident that we are ready."

"Your attendance to details in a timely manner has not gone unnoticed, Paieri."

"Beg pardon, sir," a familiar voice said. I turned to see a freckle-faced boy with large brown eyes, clean from head to toe.

"Leofrick?"

"Aye, m'lord, 'tis Frick."

"I am glad to see Paieri has seen to your needs."

"He has been most kind, m'lord, and you as well."

I smiled and turned to walk away. He ran to catch me.

"May I attend you, m'lord?" I looked over my shoulder at this lad only a few summers behind me. "Sir Plantagenet, my horsemanship should prove adequate."

"Only adequate?"

"I improved with each ride until my horse was taken from me."

"Then you must take control of another mount. What is your age, Frick?"

"Twelve summers, m'lord, near thirteen."

"While I am away, you will stay behind and work on strength and conquering your steed. Begin by taking care of my horses and cleaning stables as I once did. Paieri will go with me, so you are to do his chores and follow orders from other marshals."

"Aye, m'lord."

"Then polish my other armor and wipe down weapons I leave behind, as I once did for another." He nodded. "When I return from my journey I trust you will display adeptness in all matters."

"Aye, m'lord."

"If you are offered a chance to do mock battle, do so. You must gain strength. Implore Robert of Semblancay if you need help while we are gone. He is resourceful."

"I will, m'lord."

Jacquelin hurried to us and we all mounted our steeds, taking with us food supplies, camp tents, ample weapons of all kinds, and armor. Battles and wars fought for a king— *any* king—entangled intensely loyal and noble factions and oft times resulted in fatal treachery. My allegiance had been to my father before King Henry, but I was young and not yet a proven warrior. Now I relished battle in my father's honor in his absence, and thanked God and King Henry for my representation of The House of Plantagenet. Paieri handed me the banner signifying the Plantagenet family which I would wait to unwrap on our approach to Anjou and display in front of me to announce my arrival back in my homeland.

I kneed Honor and led the way across the bridge, Blou, Hardouin, Jacquelin, and Paieri with pack horses the train behind me, all of us in high spirits. I glanced back, thinking the king had already enlightened Matilda as to my assignment. I felt no need to see her. I grabbed my nose as we passed the stench of the market butcher, the smells off-putting, carcasses stripped of skin enough to banish my appetite for meat the rest of the day. Cleavers snapped and chopped as I hastened by. We skirted puddles of mud and muck and then galloped towards the coast past green pastures filled with lowing cows.

We ascended hills and forded streams, hastening towards the channel before the gloaming stopped us for the night. Paieri set about caring for the horses at a river that ran through forests. Jacquelin fetched water and wood to cook. Blou, Hardouin and I erected camp tents and Jacquelin's cook tent in a clearing. I sat down to watch yellow broom blooms playing through the fields up to lush green trees.

"Should I snip you a bloom, Sir Geoffrey?"

"I will fetch it myself, Hardouin." I jumped up and ran into the field, selecting a perfect bloom for my hat.

"The name Plantagenet is well-suited to you, my lord," Jacquelin said with a smile and a nod.

After a night of pleasant weather, an oppressive heat bore down on us and we moved at a sluggish pace overland. Forests thinned and ended, opening up the road to the coast. We trudged through marshland and neared the harbor where a harbinger from the king had arranged our passage.

"There she is, my lord!" shouted Hardouin. At the sight of the long ship we advanced with swiftness and boarded as oarsmen took their places. Channel waters were choppy but with a good wind behind us, we sailed to Normandy at great speed, but having difficulty when a sudden storm steered us upon rocks and tore a gap in the end of the ship. We were near enough to shore to take to horse and reach the safety of solid ground. We fared better than the damaged long ship, now no longer seaworthy.

Once we unloaded what could be salvaged from the ship, we rode hard until a fog settled over the field we crossed and slowed our pace. Our horses cantered and we came to a halt to wait out the mist. The season was changing and the air was damp and cool. A stiff wind arose and whipped at the fog, shaping into a hag before making our way clear again. But rain soon blew into our faces, drops hitting hard.

"'Tis hail! We must protect ourselves and our mounts."

We gathered under an escarpment and waited for the worst of the storm to pass before trotting on.

Honor breasted high ground and all others in the train followed. We halted at the peak and I could feel my smile reach from one ear to the other. Anjou lay ahead. I jerked Honor's reins and we descended the hill to ride beside the Maine River bank until we reached the ford and crossed. We stopped to let the horses and ourselves drink cold clear water and rest before we mounted up again to finish our journey upward to the high castle.

Grasses of green carpeted fields spread out before us as far as I could see, only a few brush trees interrupting my vision. But even though the land was ripe for grazing, I could find no creatures there. As we rode closer to my homeland, I saw the havoc wreaked by battle. Riding into the countryside near Anjou, the sight ahead left me speechless. Homes were partially burned or piles of black ash, and food crops had been trampled. The uprising seemed worse than I had thought.

We passed through my own forlorn lands, now barren— beaten down and scorched, leaving brown earth, ash and dust. I stopped and unfurled the colors of The House of Plantagenet and raised the standard. An intensified anticipation, keen excitement, and even a flurry of fear skittered through my body. I had never been in real battle. I had never felt a dagger's pierce or the slice of a sword. I had never held the standard to announce my arrival. I drew in a slow breath. Pride at representing my family knitted with the apprehension welling inside me at the same time.

"To armor, my lord?" I looked around at my men, all from somewhere in the duchy and all no doubt wondering about their families and lands.

"Not yet, Blou. Let us first see what is amiss."

Wind howled down the river below the castle at Loches, obliterating the last orange and brown leaves clinging to trees on either side of the river. Summer came to an abrupt end. Honor chuffed and squirmed, taxed as were other mounts and their riders.

Father John, wearing his official cassock, greeted us with apprehension at my father's castle door.

"Sir Geoffrey, I am pleased to see you and your men arrived whole."

"'Tis good to be home but not in these troubling times."

Father John shook his head. "Come. A meal is prepared and waiting for you. Please follow me and I will enlighten you."

After washing our hands we prayed, drank mead and ate cheese and clusters of grapes around the open fireplace. "What causes so much discontent, Father?"

"Since your father Fulk V and Lady Melisende left Anjou for Jerusalem and have not returned, and you, Count of Anjou, are living abroad in England, a number of nobles have taken an iron fist to vassals around their castles, and nobles who loathe each other quarrel like unruly imps."

"Nobles have always quarreled, Father John. But what of the ill treatment of vassals?"

"Nobles rule as little kings here. They feud with each other and with barons. Vassals attack lords and lords make war on vassals. Dukes and counts attack each other throughout the duchy unless they join forces to oppose the king himself. Nobles are restless and power-hungry with a constant urge to do battle. They heap more menial duties on peasants and vassals and take more from them. Peasants have children who are starving. Greed has set upon this place, I fear, and peasants are retaliating in growing numbers. As nobles become more agitated, they attack each other more fiercely, and word is that they oppose Fulk's hold on Anjou. That makes you unwelcome here in your own homeland, Sir Geoffrey." He touched my forearm. "I have taken the liberty to have your food tested before you eat."

"I see. Ruling from a great distance lacks control." I shook my head slowly. I had never needed someone to taste food before I ate of it.

Could someone want to poison me? A noble who cheered for me and celebrated my marriage to the king's daughter? Anger crept into my body and I clenched my wrists.

Father John continued. "Clashes between the nobles have destroyed homes and crops and many peasants have died not only in Anjou but all over Normandy. Nobles— many who are cowards—strike and retreat to the cover of their castles, leaving peasants and vassals with little or no defense. A corn stalk is no defense against a sword. And I must hasten to add that other counties of the king's domain are discontented."

"Ah. 'Tis much domain to manage." I touched his shoulder and looked him in the eye. "I saw my *own* lands in distress."

"Indeed. Your land, Sir Geoffrey, has seen overuse for many summers. Much of it lies fallow, but what crops were sown discontented peasants trampled so that distrustful merchants could not reap payment."

"I will meet with the nobility of Anjou and settle this dispute. Merchants and tradesmen are to attend as well. I remain Count of Anjou, after all."

"I wish you utmost success, my lord, but take heed. Your presence here is known by all. The duchy is in dissension. A fortnight ago, the pope and those of us in clergy decreed that all wars must stop from Thursday eve 'til Monday dawn, but we have had no good fortune with nobles. I must confess we have hidden ourselves from the fray."

"Can you return safely to your quarters then?"

"I will use the castle's underground tunnel to avoid danger," he whispered near me and bowed. "I will leave you now. God's blessing upon you all."

My barons and I, weary and famished, feasted on fresh bread, venison, and fish stew from the River Maine before setting a plan of military action. I sopped the last of my broth with bread and swallowed it down, contemplating our next move. I could ill afford to irk barons and merchants of Anjou but neither could I allow crops that fed the county to be ruined and people who relied on my leadership to be cheated and injured.

Later in the evening, a young squire brought a message from Father John that some nobles would meet with us at the following day's light. My men and I fashioned a plan to assure ourselves we were not entering an ambush from hilltops surrounding us. We inspected our weapons before bidding each other a fair rest. Inside Loches heavy gates and doors were boarded and bolted.

✤ ✤ ✤

Hardouin and Blou left the castle first to make certain we would not be targets for arrows once we left the wall. I hated to think nobles I had grown up with would do me harm, but caution was a wiser choice than pompous confidence. When my soldiers gestured for us, Jacquelin, Paieri and I stepped from the castle's protection into unfiltered sun and onto a path that led into the town's street. We walked with heads up, our eyes scouring hills and the spire of the monastery, seeing barons and other nobles filing into a side door, no archers could be seen at the ready.

Once we were inside the monastery, Father John motioned for my small band of men to sit at the head table, as after all, I was Count of Anjou. I tried to hide the fact I no longer felt in control of my own county as nobles congregated at tables on a lower level and merchants and tradesmen behind them at the back of the hall.

"I will only sit in this higher place to see and hear all of you, not because I am Count of Anjou and the representative of the Duke of Normandy and King of England." I waved my arms. "We are all of nobility and I respect that."

"Aye, my lord," many responded in unison. I looked about in hopes of finding the disgruntled faces that surely must be among them, but their true countenance was hidden from me.

Father John motioned to the vicar, who announced, "Let us unite in prayer that God be with us as we listen to one another, that a settlement may come forth that is fair and pleasing to all concerned."

We prayed together and broke fast, a taster behind me and each of my men to assure no disaster befell us. Once we had enjoyed our meal, I asked individual nobles to stand and speak their concerns.

Richard, Baron of Lyon, spoke for many: "My lord, Sir Geoffrey Plantagenet, as we have no person in control here—you and your father are abroad in distance countries—we as nobles of power have become the ruling party, not through political desire but necessity."

Many nobles bobbed their heads and uttered words of agreement.

"What necessity?"

Charles, Baron of Grenoble stood. "My lord, barons from near and far are being tested by their vassals. They do not adhere to feudalism as set forth by Fulk V and Henry, the King of England and Duke of Normandy. We have taken strong measures to assert our noble rank and they resist us at every turn."

"I see homes have been burned and crops trampled," I declared. "Do you hope to gain control again by destroying their meager livelihood, crops that feed your *own* families far better than they feed their own?" Heads drooped. "I ask you, noble gentlemen, is force the answer?"

Silence became whispering and bickering. I then spoke with an imposing voice.

"What say you, Richard of Lyon?" I turned in another direction. "Charles of Grenoble?"

"Vassals must not overstep their rank, sir!" Charles called back at me. "Lands were granted from us to them in return for an oath of fidelity and a pledge of military service. Instead *they* destroy crops and hurt not only themselves but the rest of us."

William, Count of Ponthieu shouted, "Nor must merchants and tradesmen overstep *their* positions all over the duchy." He motioned towards men at the back of the room. "Have you the answer there in your pretty golden red head, Geoffrey, *Count* of Anjou?"

I did not miss the lack of respect in his address or nods of many heads as he spoke. The hair on the nape of my neck stiffened. I had found the true enemy—the initiator of the revolt.

I forced restraint by speaking through clenched teeth. "My barons and I will discuss the matter and mayhap meet with vassals before an answer can be determined. I ask that you men refrain from further aggression in the meantime. Are we in accordance?"

Nobles whispered and nodded until William of Ponthieu spoke again. "We agree to refrain from destruction and war until Wensday next. We promise nothing further."

My men gathered beside me. "Godspeed!"

"Godspeed, Sir Geoffrey Plantagenet," the gallery called out to us as we followed Father John out.

At the door he tugged my arm. "I am pleased with your leadership, my lord. You are no longer a boy. Manhood becomes you but this discontent will sorely test your mettle. Deceit and cunning are alive and well." I nodded at him. "May God go with you," he said as he closed the monastery door behind us.

"Now to gather peasants and vassals willing to talk with us," I said to my men.

Our task proved difficult, for vassals had lost faith in their lords and in their counts, I among them. Some may have thought me to blame for the burnings and tramplings. I had to assure them that such was not the case. Gathering peasants proved to be as tiresome as chasing flying squirrels through a forest of tall trees. We devised a plan to separate and peacefully corner a few of them as they worked, thus giving them a voice in the solution.

I dressed in clothing far beneath my rank and set out alone to learn more about the fray in which I now found myself without giving away my true identity. I came upon a peasant covered in soot, making charcoal amid the undergrowth of a coppice.

"May I have a word, good fellow?"

The peasant looked over the horse I had borrowed from Father John and then at me.

"You ride a horse and have means to clothe your body. If I stop work I and my family will perish."

"I asked one question. Can you not work and answer?"

The dirty man sighed and looked about him. "We suffer many enemies and the worse men are secretive. Be you one of them?" He looked into my eyes which I kept transfixed upon his own.

"I assure you I am no enemy," I said with emphasis.

"No enemy is so difficult to guard against as the enemy at home, and 'tis this enemy we dare not resist." His hand began to tremble as though he wished to take back his words.

I dismounted in hopes of calming his fear. "What of the count? Does he not control and protect this place?"

"I speak no ill of the count or the king but they are abroad and not in this land. Wicked deeds are done under the guise of obedience to them."

"Who mistreats you?"

He looked about him again. "Shire reeves, baliffs and other servants of our lord the count. When he comes to the castles here, his servants seize goods on credit without prayer or praise. The count leaves and creditors seek repayment. The bastards then deny owing anything or defer payment 'til creditors accept a pittance."

"Then dishonest men rule."

"Aye, sir. Shire reeves go out after harvest and place an exaction on crops," the man added, glancing around. "They take advantage of the power their position gives them for their own financial gain. Many fear them."

"You among them."

The man's face reddened. "I dare say no more except that they are careful to conceal their deeds from the count." I now saw fear in his eyes and decided I had learned enough. Thanking him, I dropped a coin in his filthy hand and rode away, never admitting I was the count of whom he spoke.

6

A sinnight passed before my barons and I convened again with nobles and merchants, this time upon my invitation to Loches Castle as a show of my faith that an agreement could be reached. The hall noise began as a hum and grew into a rattling roar with demands, challenges, threatening words and angry eyes throughout, even shire baliffs taking part. Rebellion was afoot. Of that no doubt remained, order lost until I leapt upon the table's top and spread my arms to them.

"Enough!" my voice boomed.

Noblemen and merchants alike turned towards me, many with loathing or contempt in their eyes. I made a particular effort to look at sheriffs who were in charge of conduct in the county.

"We must settle our disputes with no violence. Put away your daggers and anger for the good of all. Shire baliffs, I enlist you to keep peace in this place."

Godfroi of Anjou curtly nodded his understanding at me with a tight face.

Charles of Grenoble spoke first. "The king of England and Duke of Normandy requires much of us! And if we do not make account, he sends men like *you* to punish us!"

Richard of Lyon stood. "And *you*, Geoffrey, Count of Anjou, were once one of us!"

"I am still Count of Anjou and I am *still* one of you. I have not abandoned you and I am *not* here to punish you. My father, now King of Jerusalem, has not abandoned you. We will find appeasement together but we must do so without shouting and violence. I will hear every complaint, but let us be civil in so doing. I will order a feast and much wine once we have come to agreement. King Henry seeks justice for all of you. He is distraught over the uprising that began with fraudulent hands on this soil, hands of men who put blame on the king. We must find the frauds and settle this dispute or fear the king himself will come with force!"

Many men sat down and began to whisper to each other, calmer or mayhap more calculating in their demeanor. I remained where I was and continued to speak.

"What will you merchants do without crops? What of livestock? Think on these things. I, as Count of Anjou, will come to my county posthaste and with regularity, but I must demand fair care of the county's lands, wildlife, vassals and peasants in my absence. If we cannot reach that agreement, I will send to England for mailed knights to arrest any noble who rebukes my authority on behalf of the king!"

I pointed to our weapons and armor, locking my eyes on Ponthieu. My voice thundered and became unrecognizable to me. My cheeks felt hot with anger. Whispers ended and the room quieted before I continued in a softer voice.

"You must treat these people better unless you yourselves are willing to do the labor it takes to feed your families and livestock. I see no man here willing to spend every day in mud and mire with little to show for it."

Squirming became noticeable about the hall.

"No centralized administration exists here to regulate itself in the king's absence. We have no uniform system of laws from shire to shire," I pointed out. "The same is true in weights and measures used in the marketplace. My investigation revealed wide-spread cheating, and thus, bickering and fighting have erupted. Peasants and vassals toil from morn to the gloaming and feel robbed for their efforts." I stepped from the higher level and stood in front of tables of barons, dukes, and earls. "Many of you feel robbed by merchants there in the back as well."

A slight ruckus turned all accusing eyes towards the back of the room.

"I am not accusing *any* man here. We simply have no fair system. For that the king, my father, and I will take blame. Therefore, there must be put into place fair accounting practices, for when there are disputes, Normandy suffers. I place that responsibility on each shire's seneschal and baliff." Again I looked straight at Godfroi of Anjou. "I will appoint Roger of Salisbury as Exchequer, and he will organize a fair and efficient collection of royal revenues and administer a firm hand against fraud and cheating in every transaction. He will arrive from England in a fortnight and reside at this castle until order is assured. He will hold sessions twice a year for sheriffs who collect accounts and handle financial disputes in order to curb errant officials. This procedure ensures that the king receives his income and makes the sheriff account in detail for the fairness to all subjects. Roger of Salisbury is considered a man of highest integrity in all the realm." Some heads nodded, but not all. I moved about the room so I could study faces as I spoke.

"Pipe rolls will provide a glimpse of the character of royal administration, a record of recurrent revenue from land along with an account of debts arising from agreements with individual men. Royal justices will oversee the Pipe rolls and safeguard the king's interests as well as your own. Still a good deal of local policing will remain in the hands of local lords. Know that you will be held to account. Fealty to the Crown is our first responsibility."

Men began to whisper among themselves.

I hurried on. "I own many fields, flocks, foals, herds, and forests in this county. I want peace for myself and for every man in this county and across the duchy, regardless of his rank."

"But my lord—"

"Fait accompli!" I shouted, causing a reverberation in the hall. My cheeks heated again.

Even though the nobility of Anjou begrudgingly accepted my plan, we left Normandy—giving Honor a rest while I rode Warrior—and headed back to England on a cold wind with the knowledge that all was not well. Another uprising was imminent. I was aware that while nobles might pay homage to King Henry—no more than a mark of alliance—they felt no obligation to him. Unless I stayed, all effort would be for nought, but I had sworn an allegiance to King Henry and married his daughter.

We climbed hills on rested mounts and full bellies and made good pace as land flattened ahead. We hurried past grazing cows and slowed as the road sloped again, taking us near a patch of thick brambles that appeared to reach out to claw at horses' legs and our own. Down another slope we stopped on the bank of a river before darkness set upon us.

"Paieri, see to these tired mounts. Jacquelin, fetch firewood. Blou, Hardouin and I will set up the tent and fish for our supper."

Blou laughed heartily. "Fish lock their jaws when Hardouin goes near water."

"I can catch one ere you, Blou, the smart arse," replied Hardouin with a scowl on his face.

Blou had been right about my military adviser, but fish bit no better for any of us. Jacquelin, being more resourceful, put together a decent meal before we all lay down and fell fast asleep.

I awoke at dawn's first light to whispering nearby.

"Be still, I say," Hardouin's voice was barely recognizable. "I'll take her."

I cranked open my eyes and looked in the direction of their arrows. A stout doe grazed on the other bank and twitched her ears as if hearing them, but she remained still. The arrow hit its target and the two men scampered into the river to retrieve the meat we would eat during the rest of our journey back to England. Jacquelin unmade the meat and stored it for the pack horses to carry.

Cold wind angrier than yester eve invaded every part of my body as we journeyed on, all of us blanketed beyond recognition to any other traveler we might meet. I shivered until I thought my bones would snap apart and wrapped myself tighter in the wool cloak.

As we crossed the English Channel, my stomach tied itself in knots—not from seasickness, but from the knowledge that likewise all was not well in England.

7

Once back on English soil, we stopped at a shitbrook and even though our horses and ourselves were weary, traveled on through small towns and hamlets located between us and the king's castle. A mist appeared and began to swirl and pull away from the tree line, encircling our train.

"What foul is this?" Blou called out. We all drew our swords, anticipating trouble. I turned to the others but they had disappeared in the fog as it grew more dense.

"Blou? Hardouin?" A gust of wind blew on me and the old witch returned and showed herself in clothes as ragged as her teeth.

"Man of Broom, remember," the squeaky voice uttered in a whisper.

"Remember, Man of Broom!" yelled another voice, making me jerk and startling Warrior. He stamped and blew and I held the reins tighter, looking about me, eyes wide.

"Gloom and doom for Man of Broom," came voices of several harbingers of doom at once.

As suddenly as the mist had rolled in, it disappeared taking the crones along with it. I glanced over at Blou and Hardouin who seemed not to have heard or seen what I had. The mist had dampened me, but more the reappearance of the hags had dampened my spirit further.

I prodded Warrior and galloped before my men to the brow of a hill, only then looking back at a clear field with no mist, no fog and no apparitions. Nevertheless, uneasiness settled over me as we rode on towards the castle in silence.

We reached the bridge to the Palace at Westminster, crossed and dismounted at the wall. Paieri took the reins of my horse.

"Hardouin and I will unpack, my lord," Blou said.

"I am grateful to you men. I hope our visit proved useful, but I fear we must return soon with greater force. Prepare for it," I spoke. The men dipped their heads.

Frick ran to greet us, a grin spread wide across his young face.

"My lords! I have taken good care of the horses and stable and all weapons are polished with precision," he announced with pride.

"Good. Now help Paieri, Hardouin, and Blou with our steeds for we are all in need of nourishment and rest."

"Aye, m'lord."

I left my men and entered the long hall, walking towards my private bedchamber.

"My lord," a servant called after me. "I will draw water for your bath, sir."

"My greatest wish at this moment, Godfrei."

"Sir Geoffrey, your lady wife wishes to see you."

"Ah, I will attend to her while you warm my bath." My head ached and my stomach growled but I walked to her chamber door and rapped. A lady-in-waiting opened it. I looked at my lady wife sprawled on a long tufted chaise, her long hair arranged on top of her head under a beaded wimple.

"My husband, you return," she said with iciness. "Stench of horse and dung arrived in the chamber ahead of you." She smirked at me. Her piercing words infuriated me. Her voice, rough and loud, bounced off stone walls.

I approached her with a stomp, my face heated, my heart pounding, my fist tight and ready to strike, but as my arm trembled to connect, I forced it down to my side and held it in place.

"You would strike me, Geoffrey?" Her tone was of surprise laced with challenge. Her mouth formed a defiant sneer.

I glanced at the women attending her. "Leave us!" I yelled. They ran from the room, their skirts flapping as they went.

Matilda heaved herself to her feet, her face flushed with anger, her swan neck crimson.

"Taunt me not! I am heir to the throne of England! I will be queen!"

"Cease your braying!" my own voice reverberated.

I lifted her empty chaise and jammed it into the stone wall. Then I marched to her dressing tables and raked her vanity of products onto the floor with a crash and an after effect of dust.

"You destroy my rare powders!"

I turned an angry red face to her. "Fret not, Matilda, for you are a beauty on the outside. Powders and rouges will do you no good unless you swallow them!"

She lunged at me and I spun away and watched her land on the floor, her skirts billowing over her back.

"I have been about the king's business abroad, assuring that you will have lands to reign, but I had rather war in foreign countries than battle in my own domain. I will not tolerate your insolence further, Matilda! I am your husband and you will no longer vex me at every turn in matters of state or on my appearance or performance." I neared her face. "You taunt *me* not!" My loud words echoed in the chamber as a bitter taste invaded my mouth. "Your hurtful words are meant to provoke, Matilda. Admit it!"

I shoved her back on the bed, this time with repugnance. No gentleness remained in me, only fury and a need to relieve it. I threw her skirts over her head and muffled her cries as I rammed my sweaty member into her flesh. I continued to hold the fabrics over her face, mayhap hoping to smother her while I viciously pumped into her. I knew not until that moment I possessed so much loathing for her.

Once I completed my unspeakable deed, my lady wife lay speechless for the first time since we wed, staring at me in disbelief. I pulled her skirts down, turned my back on her and left, slamming the heavy door behind me for good measure. A feeling of disgust overtook me and I stopped my stomping and shook my head. I could not believe what I had done.

Had all reason abandoned me?

A hot bath made me sweet-smelling. Anger leached out of my body and into the water, leaving me exhausted and ready for slumber. But my dastardly reaction to my lady wife stayed on my mind far longer until sleep provided the escape I needed.

✣ ✣ ✣

Days passed before I saw my lady wife again, both of us avoiding each other at meals and meditations. A tap on my chamber door stirred me in the darkness before dawn. I answered not but lifted my head as the door opened. I felt for my dagger.

"My husband?" came a whisper.

I roused. "Matilda?" I saw her face in the dim candlelight she held.

"'Tis I. May I join you . . . to talk, my lord husband?"

I sat up and leaned on the head board, drowsy and confused. She came to the edge of the bed and smiled at me, a pleasant countenance unlike any I had seen on her face; yet I kept a hand on my dagger.

"'Tis cold here."

I did not reach out to her. "Why have you come, Matilda?"

"I am your lady wife. You are my husband, Geoffrey. I have been wicked to you." I sat up straight and looked at her before I lowered my head in shame.

"No, 'tis *I* who have been wicked. And a bath *was* needed after that long journey," I admitted. "My actions cannot be taken back. I must learn to better arrest my anger. I lived not up to my best self."

"I have taken council. I have much to confess. We can only produce heirs by togetherness, Geoffrey, and the task seems difficult indeed." She looked away. "I provoked you willingly and with intent. For that I must take account." I threw coverlets back and she set the candle aside and joined me in warmth. She shifted beside me. "I do not behave well in your presence and in the presence of my ladies. 'Tis not *you* I abhor so much as the circumstances in which I find myself. You did nought to deserve my insult, Geoffrey." She shook her head. "But alas, I am but a pawn in my father's hands. My life is not my own."

"You did nought to deserve my violation, Matilda. I pray for God's forgiveness and yours."

"You are forgiven, Geoffrey. I pray not to cling to past grievances. The past is gone and will never come again."

A silence filled the room as we lay there with some distance between us.

"I know."

"*Do* you know?" Her voice held surprise and she swung her head in my direction. "What know you, Geoffrey?"

"Your father, King Henry, told me of your once high position. I am sorry for the loss of the emperor and all other losses you endured in the aftermath of his death. You were forced into this marriage of ours. Perchance if your father had sought a mate of higher status, you would be happy. I cannot imagine what it must be like to wed an emperor as a child and have high status through the realm and then to marry a 'mere count.'"

"Oh, Geoffrey, 'tis true that in a lower status I found myself. I hold immense resentment, but 'tis no fault of yours." She turned towards me. "Can you forgive *me*? My haughtiness? My constant rudeness? Can we mend our frayed bond?"

"What hoax is this? Is that what you wish, or is this wicked trickery?"

"Geoffrey!" She shifted herself to the edge of the bed, became silent for a while before she sighed heavily. "I earned that remark," she muttered, easing back towards me. "'Tis not trickery. I am sincere in wanting to make amends for the king, my father, and bear his heirs. I am praying as well. We must find a way."

"I have been trying and willing, Matilda, but I cannot muster much enthusiasm to touch you even though you are beautiful." I took careful measure before I spoke again. "Your unrelenting insolence is undeserved."

"'Tis true. I know not from whence my foulness comes, my husband. It springs forth at the most inopportune times."

"I always end frustrated and limp."

"I will coax you," she whispered. "But you must hold your Plantagenet ire with me."

"And you, my lady wife, must hold your tongue."

"But, my lord," she said, throwing the coverlet aside and untying my braies, "can I not use my tongue in other ways?" I removed my hand from the dagger and held her in my arms. An excited but gentler serpent coiled in my braies.

✤ ✤ ✤

The next dawn, after prayers, I had five horses at my disposal and chose carefully. Nutmeg, a strawberry roan, I used for personal recreation. He was not large or fit for battle but preferred a slow gait on a path of briars and brambles down the hill from the castle when we had time. My dextriers—Lord and Count—were war horses. My highly-prized Arabians—Warrior and Honor—I saved for a display of all-out warfare. They were strong enough to run full out with a knight dressed in full metal and weapons, but I knew I needed to devote more attention to getting accustomed to them and them to me. When the call to war came, it would be those two who took me into it and brought me safely home again.

At the stables I roused my squire from his bed.

"Frick! Up at once!"

The boy scrambled up, his head a tousled mass of curls. "What goes on, m'lord?"

I had to snicker at his wide eyes and unkempt mane "Do you think you can ride a horse and see where you go, Frick?"

"Surely, sir. I have been practicing when I could, although taking care of stables and keeping your weapons polished takes much time."

"Prepare Nutmeg for you and Warrior for me. And make no mistake or we will spill in the countryside."

"Aye, m'lord!"

I checked the reins and bits before we strolled across the bridge and out in the country away from town. Once we had a clear path, I popped Nutmeg on the flank and he galloped off with Frick hanging on, wild hair in the breeze. Warrior stayed with Nutmeg, under my control. I wanted the headstrong horse to learn who was in charge for I must be sure of him or we would both perish. Frick and I rode until sun glared in our eyes and we came to a stop beside one another.

"Sir Geoffrey, 'tis a fine horse, and the one you ride is finer still." He rubbed Nutmeg's ears and grinned at me.

"I will be called to war anon, Frick, and I expect you to take care of Nutmeg and the others who stay behind."

"Oh, sir, can I go with you to battle?"

"No," I said, mayhap a little strong. Frick's head dropped. "You are young. I am barely old enough for war myself. Yet I am wed and a knight who took an oath to protect. Once you demonstrate adeptness in handling the horses and mayhap setting camps, you can accompany us on excursions requiring no full combat."

"Thank you, m'lord. I will work hard and prove my worth, sir."

"I have no doubt." I trotted off towards the castle, looking back long enough to say, "Prove yourself and Nutmeg is yours."

I trotted away from him. Hearing his shouts of joy behind me lifted my spirits to a higher plane.

8

Matilda and I settled into a routine of less-conflicted marital duties although it bewildered me that my lady wife seemed to need constant encouragement from the wine cellar. Nevertheless, after frequent coupling, Matilda sent for the royal physician who examined her in private and announced to her father and me that Matilda was with child. King Henry was ecstatic and I was proud and relieved. Now the hope was for an uneventful term and a healthy heir—preferably male.

An heir! I floated on air towards the door, realizing the significance of the news. But even though Matilda was relieved, her demeanor towards me changed that very night when she became brittle in my embrace.

"Are you not happy? What troubles you?"

"We have an heir on the horizon. I will not need you to service me further, Geoffrey."

The bite in her voice startled me. I extricated my body from hers. "Service you?" My anger grew; I felt my face redden. "I am no more than a *service* to you?"

She stared at me. "Distress me not, Geoffrey. Go and busy yourself elsewhere. Get to your jousts and tournaments," she said, touching her finger to her chin in thought, "but first, go hunting. I want to dine on swan." She dismissed me with a wave of haughty indignation as though our rutting had meant nought to her. I found this sudden flash of animosity both disturbing and galling but even her foul disposition could not mar my exhilaration on this day.

✤ ✤ ✤

At dawn's first light, I strutted to the stables, hearing the crow of roosters and the cries of fishmongers from the town below as I went. I called out to my squire.

"To horse at once!"

He ran past me with a quick bow and nod. "Which, m'lord?"

"Saddle Count," I responded. After hesitating, I added, "And Nutmeg for you."

The boy grinned. "Aye, m'lord!"

I looked from whence he had come and spotted the beginnings of a tree saddle. I walked to it. "'Tis your work, Frick, or the work of Paieri?"

"'Tis mine, m'lord," he replied with a reddened face.

"A fine beginning. I knew not of your talent."

"'Tis not done yet, m'lord, but I am about it once all chores are done."

"Then let us attend to our first chore of the day. My lady wife wishes to dine on swan." My voice, perchance, gave away my repugnance at my lady wife's request, and my squire eyed me with curiosity and shrugged.

"What of my chores, sir?"

"Pages and grooms will attend to your duties 'til we return," I said, nodding at a group of boys who gathered at the stable doors.

My squire and I mounted and rode across fields now harvested towards the far pond where swans were known to breed and nest, the air full of promise of a changing season. I spurred Count and Nutmeg kept pace, Frick clinging to him with a grimace.

"Let them loose," I shouted as the horses took us swiftly to the water's edge. We dismounted and tethered the mounts to a bramble bush. One large swan neared us, the others far down the bank on the other side of the pond.

"Frick, swim out and head off the beast while I close in behind," I called out to the boy.

He looked at me with hesitation. "Go into the water, m'lord?"

I nodded and tried to hide my grin. If the lady wife wanted a swan, she would have it if my squire could best the creature himself. I half-heartedly waded into water but stayed back to see what my squire could do alone. He had rid himself of boots and coat and swam far out and circled back towards the swan. The bird turned back towards the bank but stopped at the sight of me, turned downstream and swam with speed. Frick tried to close the distance while I ran along the embankment.

"Hasten, Frick, hasten!" I slammed into a thicket of briars and had to get back into the water as the swan zipped around and headed straight for my squire, its beak ready for attack.

"Watch yourself, Frick!" I yelled just as the large bird struck him in the nose. He clambered towards the bank as it struck again and pulled himself up partway before slipping in mud and rolling back into water. The swan spun and swam away, honking as I threw back my head and laughed with great enthusiasm. The laughter cleansed my ill temper.

"M'lord," Frick said as he plopped on the bank near me, "your lady wife will be sorely disappointed, I fear." He rubbed his bitten nose and wiped away blood.

"Alas, my squire, then disappointed she will be." I laughed hard enough to need to hold my aching sides as my shivering squire looked at me with great curiosity. "No worthier wild swan chase have I relished more."

I looked over my soaked and bloody squire and tossed him a cloth. "Address your wound, Frick. You have been bested by a swan." I laughed again and my squire joined me, shaking his head in feigned shame.

We hung our wet clothes on the bramble bush to dry in stiff breeze and sunshine. As we sat there waiting for them to dry, I glanced over at Frick again.

"All is not lost, my squire. The river has made you smell no more of horse dung."

He nodded and a grin spread under his red bulbous nose.

9

The first day of winter roared in with a strong cold wind whipping trees and bushes and tents and merchant stands in town. Pastured horses ran briskly with tails high, some tagging others as they romped. I was thankful to have fine shelter and plenty of firewood, although more would be needed to keep fires burning throughout the castle before winter ended. Castle stores were filled with harvested crops, among them corn meal and flour, dried apples and other fruits, lard and herbs. Meats from hunts hung in smoke. We would fare better than most of the country's people until planting season returned in spring.

Darkness crept in early and lingered long. The moon often hid itself from us. Loneliness accompanied me to my bedchamber at night. I found myself staying up late to play chess or throw darts alone or with anyone willing to pass time with me.

Paieri and Semblancay made a noisy entrance late one night. I turned.

"My lord," Paieri said with a bow. "We have just returned from purchase of the king's new mount, a splendid steed, indeed."

"He will be pleased," I said.

Semblancay stepped forward and handed me a blue velvet cloth.

"What?"

"'Tis a precious gemstone for you to give your lady wife at The Feast of Saint Nicholas," he explained.

I opened the cloth and peered at a large ruby pendant. "I am certain that such a fine gem will divert Lady Matilda's attentions from this cold harsh winter and beyond. Thank you for attending to this purchase on my behalf, Semblancay."

He bowed.

"We bid you good sleep, Sir Geoffrey," Paieri said. The men left and I stared at the bauble, twirling it between my fingertips. It would be beautiful on Matilda's long neck and mayhap, if need arose, I could enlist it to choke the last breath from her condescending body.

The weather worsened and snow drifted up castle walls as winds unleashed their fury. Inside the castle, walls and floors became colder and drearier. And more lonely. In daylight my men and I plowed open doors and the main gate to escape into the countryside for hare tracking or horse racing and to keep roads clear for the forthcoming season's guests.

The Feast of Saint Nicholas arrived and Frick, other squires, pages, and grooms brought in fresh boughs of greenery they had been sent to pluck from nearby forests for the occasion. The castellan and chatelaine gave orders as servants set about decorating the Palace and the Great Hall at Westminster. Aromas from the kitchens found my nostrils and enticed me in their direction for a morsel or two. I passed iron cauldrons of bubbling soup and spits of roasting meats in the fireplace and reached for a sweet from Jacquelin's table before he pushed my hand away.

"Save your appetite. You will need it," he said, and we both laughed.

The royal family and nobles dressed in regal clothing and feasted on oysters, pheasants and wild boar, turnips, figs and pears, and fresh breads, some savory and some sweet. Wine was poured in abundance and laughter and joviality filled the castle. Matilda and I sat at the head table with King Henry and Queen Adeliza, whom I seldom saw. She was rumored to be ill of health and stayed in her private chamber even to dine unless summoned by King Henry to make an appearance. We ate, drank and laughed cordially throughout feasting. My lady wife remained distant to me although she and her father became closer as the promise of an heir loomed on the horizon.

Matilda presented King Henry with bits of colored glass in his likeness held together with melted lead—called leaded glass—in a size that would fit one of the high chapel windows. The king beamed. I presented my lady wife with the ruby pendant—now on a chain—by slipping it on her neck myself. She seemed delighted at the size and quality. I handed her the cloth to protect it when not being worn. Music and merriment would transpire for a fortnight, gifts of spun sugar candy—no doubt made by Jacquelin—for children throughout the noble classes, for those who served in the castle, and for us.

As I moved away from the head table and watched Matilda and her attendants leave the hall, my squire cleared his throat beside me.

"Sir Geoffrey, might I have a word?"

"What is amiss, Frick?"

He pointed behind him to a leather saddle. "'Tis my gift to you, m'lord," he said with pride.

I stepped over to it and examined it from pommel to cantle. "'Tis a beautiful saddle, Leofrick. You are talented, indeed." I studied the saddle's intricate detailing and smiled broadly.

"Your work is honorable, my squire. Did you get the king's gifts?"

"I did, m'lord, and I am gratified. I have never had such a fine holiday."

"I have not a gift for you, Frick," I said, embarrassment edging onto my face.

"You have given me Nutmeg, m'lord. He is a fine mount, the likes of which I have never had. He is my gift, along with food, shelter and service to the royal family, m'lord. I want nought but to please you."

I grinned. "Can you get this saddle back to the stable and put away in a special place for me?"

"I can, m'lord."

I watched my squire lift the saddle with ease and grin at me once again before he left. As I headed down the long hall to my bed chamber, I turned a corner and collided with a beautiful woman dressed in emerald green and gold.

"Annique!"

She curtsied. "My lord."

"What brings you here?"

"You know not, my lord?" I shook my head. "Lady Matilda summoned me."

"For what purpose?"

She smiled. "I am your gift."

Stunned by her answer, I stared.

"My lord?"

"My tongue is tied," I explained, never letting my eyes leave hers.

"Mayhap I can help loosen it, my lord," she whispered seductively.

✣ ✣ ✣

In my bedchamber I pulled off my coat, belt, boots and hose before noticing steam rising from my bath water.

I glanced at Annique with curiosity.

"Lady Matilda had it drawn for you . . . us," she whispered near me.

Even though I had puzzling and mixed emotions about this arrangement, I walked over to the beauty I had missed.

"Then we must not disappoint the heir to the throne of England."

"No, my lord."

I stripped myself before unwrapping my gift and taking her to the water, lowering her into steam.

She regarded me as I leaned over her. "Your shoulders have broadened, Sir Geoffrey the Handsome. You have grown taller and more manly," she purred as I lowered myself into the water facing her. She used her foot to swirl the hair on my chest, making me hard even before her foot tiptoed lower.

"You are a fuzzy sack of plums, my lord," she said, grinning at me with mischief.

"And those plums are turning swiftly to rocks, my beautiful Annique."

We washed, dried and oiled each other with great tenderness, our passion mounting as I lifted her onto my bed.

"I have known great loneliness," I confessed without hesitation.

"For that I am aggrieved, but loneliness shall not rule *this* night, my lord."

We rutted with fierceness—but somehow, at the same time, with a certain sweetness—throughout the night, both of us insatiable.

My gift was no longer in my bed when I awoke, but my spent body knew searching for her was a fruitless effort. I lounged in bed, covers strewn around until I heard a tap on the door wrestling me from my thoughts.

"My lord?"

"Godfrei?"

"My lord? Shall I return at a later hour?"

"No, enter. I have slept late. I am alone and the bath

water is used and cold." The small man opened the door and bowed, moving towards the water.

"I will attend to this and your bed, my lord."

I hopped into my braies and the rest of my clothing before air chilled and sickened me.

"Am I late to break fast? I am famished."

Godfrei smiled at me. "You might search out Jacquelin. He saved you a sweet or two, my lord."

I passed through the kitchen, and with sweet breads in hand, I walked on to the stables in hopes of testing the saddle my squire had given me.

"M'lord?" Frick ran to me as I thrust bread in his direction. "Thank you, m'lord!"

"I have you to thank for this fine saddle." I glanced towards the field. "I see snow has started to melt. Saddle Lord and come along with me to test it." The boy dashed to fulfill my order, bread clamped firmly in his jaws as he ran.

Once through the gates, we let loose the horses—stabled for most of the winter—and they gave us an exhilarating ride over the hill to tall trees at the edge of the king's royal forest. I dismounted and rubbed my crotch.

"Is the saddle a poor fit, m' lord?"

"I am chafed. Perchance you can adjust the pommel."

"I will do my best, m'lord."

We walked our horses back to the castle, jesting and planning a day to practice archery in nearby fields.

"We must wait until winter is kinder to set up targets, Frick, but practice in the hay if you can." A wicked wind whipped around us as I gave my horse to the squire and walked inside.

10

I had seen nought of Matilda since the Feast of Saint Nicholas so I tapped on her door as I went down the hall. An attendant opened it.

"Sir Geoffrey, may I assist you?"

"Is my lady wife within?"

The lovely attendant's face reddened. "No, my lord. Do you know nought?"

"Know what?"

"She has left the castle and is on holiday, sir."

"Left the castle in this abominable weather? No, I know not of it." I came into the chamber and looked it over, lest Matilda was yet there. I turned to the lady-in-waiting. "Where is she?"

"I know not, my lord. I only know that some of her attendants are with her and Sir Richard of York."

Sir Richard?

I remained still, reckoning, before I walked towards the door, turned and studied the beauty.

"You are familiar."

"I am Adelaide of Anjou, my lord."

I looked her over. "The little imp who tormented me at play?"

She laughed and covered her mouth. "I am, my lord." Her wispy long dark honey hair framed her face, pink lips, and eyes the color of the channel.

"You have grown into an exquisite beauty, Adelaide. It does my heart good to see you here," I said softly.

"Thank you, my lord. And you are long of limb and broad of shoulder, Sir Geoffrey the Handsome." She curtsied. "I attend Queen Adeliza, but am now to attend Lady Matilda's chamber and prepare for the arrival of your child, the new heir."

"I am most distressed that my lady wife travels in this harsh season especially without me to see to her safety. I hope we meet again, Adelaide, but I must pursue Lady Matilda." I bowed to my childhood friend who had grown into a handsome woman, indeed, and wondered how she had moved from the ranks of nobility in Normandy to attendant in England. But I rushed away, wanting to learn more about my lady wife's hasty departure and the reason for it.

I met the king's chamberlain at his door. "I would have a word with King Henry." He nodded and went inside, closing the door while I waited. When the door opened, he led me to the king in his wooden tub.

I bowed. "Your Grace!"

"Geoffrey, come near." He looked at the men attending him and waved an angry arm at them. "Leave us!"

The king splashed his bath water with irritation. "You have learned of my daughter's departure from the castle."

"Just now."

"I am not able to Matilda and it seems *you* are no more adept."

"Where has she gone? She is with child out in wicked weather."

"My heir!" The king threw his bathing cloth across the room. "She sent a messenger once she left the castle to tell me she is separated from *you*."

"Sire? I know nought of this."

"Ah, Matilda's head is made of unyielding boulder. But her mother may know more. You may speak with her." The king rose from the bath, displaying his royal rotund naked body. "But Sir Geoffrey Plantagenet, I'll have your head if harm comes to my daughter or my heir! I demand that you find her and return with her to the castle." His roar rattled my bones as much as his accusing finger pointed in my direction.

"Your Grace, Matilda and I stay at odds. Our marriage is a fiasco."

"I care not! You are married and with those sacred vows you swore an oath to each other. And you, Sir Geoffrey Plantagenet, promised to always protect her."

Even though I was prepared to pack and go on pilgrimage to get away from all the ruckus and deception, I had, indeed, sworn to protect and serve. I let out a long but soft sigh and left the ill-tempered king, wishing to suppress my own ire as I approached the queen's chamber in a different segment of the palace.

The queen propped on pillows as I walked into the room. I bowed.

"Queen Adeliza, may I have a word?"

"Sir Geoffrey," she said with no emotion.

"Matilda has fled. I need to know her whereabouts so I—"

"So you can torment her more?"

"*I* torment *her*?"

"Play no games with me, Sir Geoffrey. All inside the castle are aware of your dalliance with a courtesan on the Feast of Saint Nicholas!"

I felt heat flush my face. "Queen Adeliza, my lady wife sent the courtesan as my gift." I explained.

"Why say you such?"

"The courtesan came to me. She said she was sent by Lady Matilda as my gift."

"Nonsense!" the queen shouted. "And you trust a courtesan? You have been duped, Sir Geoffrey Plantagenet. Matilda made no such arrangement and now she is God knows where in this frigid weather unfit for man or beast." She leaned towards me. "You must go and find her, Geoffrey, and bring her home at once."

"I will, my lady."

"Then Godspeed." The queen waved me away and sank into her pillows as though exhaustion had overtaken her.

✢ ✢ ✢

Blou, Hardouin, Frick and I set off on different courses into the hinterland to locate Matilda and her party, but to no avail. We searched on, widening the territory to be covered, sloshing through icy mud as we went. I asked questions and got no answers until I stopped at a market in far York and spied one of her attendants at a fruit vendor.

"Livia," I grabbed her arm and she looked up at me, startled. "Where is she? Take me there."

"Sir Geoffrey, I must not."

"I am a knight. Her husband. The father of her child. You *must*. She will blame me, not you."

She nodded and I walked with my horse beside her to a cottage outside of York, far to the west. From there I sent my squire to find Blou and Hardouin and bring them to this place.

Sir Richard of York saw our approach and placed his hand on his dagger, as I did mine.

"I want no trouble," I said as I walked closer.

Livia disappeared around Sir Richard and into the cottage.

"Lady Matilda wishes not to see you, Sir Geoffrey Plantagenet," Sir Richard announced with a deep threatening tone. "I am here to guard her."

I looked about. "What cottage is this?"

"It belongs to my family."

Wind whipped about us and I shivered. "Another snow approaches. I came to escort my lady wife back to the warmth of the Windsor Castle fires."

"'Tis warm here. She wants no part of you."

I stepped closer. "Matilda carries a part of me, the heir to the English throne. King Henry himself sent me."

"Your travel has been for nought."

I stood taller than he and lowered my face near his. "You would *dare* to keep me from my lady wife? You would *dare* rebuke the king of England?" My voice boomed with anger and birds flew farther away. I pulled my dagger.

"I must—"

"Sir Richard," we both turned as Matilda's voice came from the cottage doorway, "I will see Sir Geoffrey Plantagenet." She looked at me with a trace of a smile and her guard stood down.

I sheathed my dagger and entered the cozy cottage. Matilda's attendants donned heavy layers and went outside so that we were alone. She remained by the fire, her face radiant.

"My lady," I bowed with respect," you look well and I am thankful of it."

"It pleases me to hear those words, Geoffrey. But why have you searched me out?"

"Why, indeed. You, my lady wife, fled the castle under the cloak of darkness in most foul weather. Your health and that of our child concern me, your father and the queen."

"You have spoken to my step-mother?"

"She and the king sent me to find you and bring you home."

She turned her face towards the flame and away from me. "And *you* Geoffrey Plantagenet? What of *you*?"

I walked over and took her shoulders, turning her to face me. "I want you back in the castle." I held her and we locked eyes. "I know we are estranged even inside castle walls, but no matter what you think of me, Matilda, your health and safety are my uppermost concern. I swore an oath to protect you." She dropped her head. "Will you come with me without use of force, Matilda?"

"I will." I kissed her and backed away at her surprise. She circled me, looked me over and smirked. "Did you enjoy my gift?"

I could feel my face redden. "I know not the reason for the gift, but Queen Adeliza said *you* did not give me the gift."

She smiled. "My step-mother need not know all my secrets." She whisked around to avoid more talk of the courtesan. "I shall pack. Can we make the journey by darkness?"

"I fear not."

"Then you must stay the night."

"My men are here. I will have them set tents nearby."

"Is there room for my ladies and Sir Richard there?"

"Ample space for your ladies, Sir Richard, Hardouin, Blou and my squire."

Although Sir Richard was not content with sleeping in a tent outside his own cottage, he acquiesced, leaving Matilda and I alone. She allowed me to bed her. She was stunning and the smile and change in disposition made her more so. Desire awakened swiftly and much of the night was spent in gentle delight for both of us. We made the most of darkness with no leaning ears to hear and no prying eyes to see, Matilda at times ill at ease but more amorous than I had ever known her. When we were spent, I kissed her swelling belly and sleep overtook us.

Dawn's light woke me and I lay there looking at the face of my lady wife, still sleeping. A beautiful woman, no doubt, only .... Her sudden changes in demeanor puzzled me, but at the moment I could nought complain. She stirred beside me.

"Geoffrey?"

"You slept well," I said.

"The best in a fortnight." I leaned over and kissed her lips, just barely touching them. She smiled and hid her face from me.

"What troubles you on this new day, Matilda?"

"I . . . I have once again treated you most foul, my husband." She threw back the covers and stood. I rose and met her at the bed's foot.

"I thought you treated me well throughout darkness," I replied, giving her a warm smile.

She touched my weather-beaten face with her fingers. "Only *this* night. For many I have not. I wrestle with myself." She stroked my cheek. "I promise better, Geoffrey, to treat you as my husband—a man now, no longer a boy." She stepped away from me. "You have become a more commanding presence that I find most attractive, and you have proven yourself worthy of my respect."

I remained speechless as she moved about the room. I looked out the window to see men dismantling camp.

"We must leave, but first, I must know the reason for the gift," I said, taking her by the arm.

"My ruby is a beauty from its shiny surface to the richness of its core. I wished the same beauty for you, my husband." She sniffed. "The courtesan is quite lovely and taught you well."

"But my lady wife, *you* are the beauty, even more now with a radiant face and the posture with which you carry our child." I touched her belly with a light hand.

"Your words are tender, my husband, but are they true?"

"My words are true, Matilda," I answered with a controlled voice. Personal discontent was suppressed for the moment.

Sir Richard stayed behind at his cottage after aiding our departure and providing our train with ample food and drink. The looks he gave Matilda after offering her a heavy wrap to keep chill away were not lost on me. This knight appeared enamored with my lady wife. Secretly I felt relief that he did not travel with us.

The journey back to Windsor Castle was pleasant enough although a high brisk wind and muddy paths slowed our pace.

11

The rest of winter sequestered us in the castle as Matilda grew more anxious and uncomfortable. All those who attended her met her every whim and fancy and Queen Adeliza and I visited her daily. I spent the last days of the season mending weapons and making new ones with other knights. Frick, now apprenticed to Paieri, repaired tack and saddles. As winter began to wane, Matilda called for the royal physician, who had been given an adjoining chamber in order to watch over her.

When I heard the physician had been summoned, I ran to Matilda's bedchamber door, where Queen Adeliza stopped me short.

"Sir Geoffrey, 'tis a private matter. Contractions have begun. You may wait here in the corridor for news."

I folded my long body on the cold stone floor, listening to agonizing screams from Matilda. Sweat appeared on my brow and I tensed with each outburst and the accompanying words of comfort from Queen Adeliza I could hear through the thick door, the door that did not contain in the commotion which accompanied childbirth. I became queasy and light-headed.

The Archbishop of Canterbury arrived and was allowed into the bedchamber to witness the birth of King Henry's heir. The ritual was done to make certain the heir was in good health and not switched at birth. There could be no question of the baby's right to the throne. I, on the other hand, was not allowed entrance.

After a while a soft voice called my name. "Sir Geoffrey?"

I lifted my head from my knees and looked into Adelaide's English Channel eyes. "I brought you a morsel from Jacquelin with his kindest regards."

"I partake not of any morsel, Lady Adelaide 'til there is cause to celebrate," I whispered just as Matilda let out a screech.

"The time to celebrate will come," she said, reassuring me. She offered me a cloth-covered loaf of sweet bread. "Save this until you celebrate."

"I will, Lady Adelaide." She smiled, and walked away so quietly had I not watched after her I would have thought she floated like an angel.

Later in the day Godfrei ambled down the corridor carrying with him a heavy parcel.

"Sir Geoffrey," he greeted me and leaned down to hand me the bundle, "a new textile guild has emerged. A weaver has sent over samples for Lady Matilda to survey. He wishes to weave a tapestry for the royal nursery."

I took the parcel and tumbled it over in my hands. "I will see that my lady wife gets this. Thank him, Godfrei."

"Aye, my lord," he said with a bow and walked away.

I heard Matilda's prolonged shriek of sheer agony, followed by a robust infant's cry. I jumped to my feet, dropped the parcel and pounded on the door.

"Let me enter!"

"Patience, my lord, patience," the physician called out.

I stared at the heavy door until I heard the bolt click and the door opened.

"Sir Geoffrey Plantagenet, come and greet your son," Queen Adeliza said proudly.

I walked cautiously into the room, first checking on my lady wife whose heaving chest looked as though it would burst. "Is Matilda well?"

"Tired and relieved, but in good health," the physician said. He swaddled the infant and handed him to me.

My son!

I had never felt such love, such adoration, such relief. I could not contain my happiness. I had never held a babe in my arms, so to hold my son for the first time made gooseflesh appear all over my body. I touched his hairless head, his silky bare shoulders and unwrapped him enough to check his fingers and toes. He smelled new. His skin, though pink, was smooth and in good health. His face, though reddened, held a radiance I had never witnessed. And I was his proud father.

"Swaddle him, Sir Geoffrey, to keep the chill off," the physician said after giving me time to inspect my son. He rewrapped the baby and smiled at me. "He will be King of England one day."

I peered at him through watery eyes.

"He is exquisite, Matilda," I said as I walked over to her bed. She held out her trembling arms and I lay the baby—our perfect son and heir to the English throne—in her arms and kissed her crimson cheek, still damp with perspiration.

I heard a crier announce the birth of our son, followed by a jubilant crowd 's roar of delight and a cacophony of bells to celebrate his arrival.

12

A few mornings later after meditation and holding my son, I handed Matilda the weaver's parcel. She tore open the thick covering to look upon exotic silks and threads that could be woven into colorful combinations of purple and scarlet.

"They are sumptuous!"

I left a blissful lady wife, broke fast and headed to the stables where Paieri instructed grooms, pages, and squires. I leaned against hay until he finished and they dispersed to fulfill their assignments.

"Paieri, we have some promising young men, do we not?"

"We do, your squire by far the best of the lot."

I smiled at the marshal. "I am pleased you brought him from the dung heap."

"Leofrick is most industrious and runs rings around the others although they try to best him. He will be a leader once he ages."

"My hope, Paieri." I shook his shoulder a bit. "Now tell me, has the weather broken enough for knights to practice in the fields?"

"We can set targets for later today, Sir Geoffrey. I will inform the herald of your wishes."

"Good! Have him send a messenger to all the king's knights to join us then." Paieri moved a saddle and turned to face me. "You are now the father of a future king, Sir Geoffrey." He grinned and I returned it.

"'Tis true and I will protect him with my life," I added with emphasis.

"Then let us celebrate!" Paieri shouted.

✦ ✦ ✦

A cadre of castle knights and their squires had convened in the fields between the castle and the long forest where targets set up by the herald awaited us. After congratulating me on the birth of an heir, we focused our attention on besting each other at archery. Our quivers were filled with arrows begging to be tested. We practiced on horseback and then sent our squires to tether our mounts away from danger while we collected our arrows and lined up on foot for more practice. The day was cold, but sun and constant movement warmed us so we dared to stay outside until sunset. The air filled with the swish and thunk of arrows hitting the mark and the release of much-needed shouts and laughter.

When we returned to the castle after retrieving our last arrows and targets, I dismounted and gave Frick my horse.

"Why so long a face?"

"'Tis nothing, m'lord," he replied with a dropped head.

I studied his demeanor. "Ah, I know." I patted him on the back. "You will bring your own bow on the morrow."

"But, sir, I have no bow."

I thrust mine towards him. "Then you will have mine."

"No, m'lord. I—"

"I have others. 'Tis settled."

A grin reached his jutting ears swiftly.

❖ ❖ ❖

Hoarfrost had settled over the land on the morrow as I tapped on Matilda's chamber door. When I entered three ladies-in-waiting stirred frantically around her bed.

"What is amiss?" They turned, bowed to me and spun their attention back to Matilda, who seemed more disgruntled.

"Lady Matilda is ill-rested," an attendant whispered to me. "Young Henry cried throughout the night, my lord."

"Where is he? Is he well?"

"Aye, my lord, he is there," she pointed through adjoining doors.

Matilda clucked her tongue at me. "I am not up to a visit, my husband," she said, waving her arm crossly at me.

"I will see Henry, my son," I said sternly. I backed away from her bed and walked into the nursery, where the baby still fretted in a nursemaid's arms.

"Is he ill?"

"No, my lord. He is a babe being a babe. Lady Matilda has not the patience needed—" She stopped her words and her face reddened. "Oh, I beg your pardon sir!"

I smiled and nodded, understanding at her candor. "No pardon is needed, but I do wish to hold this fussy moppet."

I gathered the bundle in my arms and the future king quieted and looked at me with bright blue eyes. I walked to the high window's sun and looked him over. He smiled up at me and if he had not already held my heart, he stole it then.

Each day the same ritual presented itself. I went into Matilda's chamber and got a scowl and berating words for the trouble. Though the weather warmed, my lady wife's private chamber stayed frigid.

"I wish not to be bothered," she barked.

"I am here to see my son, not to bother you," I said tersely. She did not respond but looked irritated. I passed through to spend time with Henry before taking Frick out for some target practice. How I wanted my son in another arrangement so I could avoid Matilda.

But, alas, the babe should be near his mother, I suppose.

✤ ✤ ✤

"No, Frick," I said, taking the arrow from him. "You must nock it into the string like this." I demonstrated. "Now you try."

My squire did not have the strength to pull the arrow back and it fell to the ground, much to his embarrassment.

"Strength will come with age. Do not distress."

He continued to nock the arrow but he could not pull the taut string back far enough. "I will practice 'til I master archery, m'lord."

"Of that I have no doubt."

Frick's arrows fell spent before they reached the target. He emptied his quiver and hastened to pick them up and try again.

"Might I offer that you move closer to the target? You are far away. Once you master closer, then you can put more distance between."

He walked up a few steps, nocked the arrow and released it, hitting the target for the first time. Elated with a smear of confidence, he landed all arrows on the edge of the marked hide.

"You have done well, my squire. Now let us get about our other duties before nightfall."

I walked swiftly away towards Windsor Castle.

❖ ❖ ❖

"How are you resting?" I asked my lady wife. "Young Henry seems to be thriving."

"Indeed he is. And sleeping the night," she said with a forced smile.

I stepped closer to her chaise.

"Why are you here, Geoffrey?"

I stopped in place. "In the bedchamber? Why, to see young Henry . . . and you," I sputtered out as an afterthought.

"The nursemaid has taken him to the chapel sun."

"Ah." I lowered my head in disappointment before looking her over. "Would you like to take a walk on this beautiful warm day? You have been inside the castle since—"

"Since you brought me home from York," she said tartly. "No, I do not wish to walk. I did so earlier. Now I am content to be here *alone*." Even though the air outside warmed, her words became icicles in the room she occupied.

I bowed. "Then it will please me to leave you to yourself and visit our son later." I headed down the long hall, but stopped and changed course, deciding to check on my son in the chapel. When I neared him, I recognized who held him.

"Lady Adelaide?" She whirled and startled Henry, who wailed. "I never meant to startle you or my son."

"'Tis wise to let us know you are coming from a distance away, Sir Geoffrey," she said, smiling up at me. She settled Henry who soon dozed in the sunny spot she had found.

"For what purpose do you attend him?"

"The nursemaid fell ill and I offered to watch him, my lord. He is a precious child." She gazed upon him with the devotion his mother should own.

"He is." I sat down on the pew beside her to watch him sleep. To be so near lovely Adelaide caused my groin to tingle with an undeniable charge. "Do you have duties all night, Adelaide?"

She gently rocked my son. "No, my lord. I will be relieved at sunset," she whispered looking over at me. Our eyes locked. "I am free then until the morrow."

"Where do you bed?" I asked boldly.

"A room adjoins the queen's private chamber. 'Tis not spacious but 'tis enough, and I am glad to have it."

I cleared my throat. "May I see you later?"

"Where, my lord?"

"Come to my private chamber and we can revisit our childhood memories."

❖ ❖ ❖

Sunset came and darkness behind it, but I did not hear a rap on my door. Mayhap I had been too bold in asking her to come. I paced and felt foolish, wishing I had applied more subtlety in arranging a visit with Lady Adelaide. Perchance I had frightened her and would never be close to her again. I drank wine and paced more. I warred with my emotions as darkness came. I pulled back the covers of my bed and lifted a leg to slide in when I heard a light tap on the door.

Easing to it, I asked, "Who goes there?"

"'Tis I," came a sweet low voice.

I opened the door and pulled her into the room, looking both ways to determine if prying eyes watched from down the hall.

"I am unhindered, my lord. The queen wanted a hot bath and requested I attend her," Adelaide explained. She looked apprehensive dressed in a velvet gown the color of the sky on a cloudless day, a ruby red belt tied around her tiny waist.

"Duty first," I said, smiling down at the petite beauty. "I am happy prying eyes did not see you at my door." Awkwardness filled the space between us. "May I offer you a sip of wine?"

"Wine would be most pleasant, my lord."

We sat on chairs near the open hearth although only embers remained. Even though summer approached, sunlight never reached my private chamber and stone walls held in dankness.

"As nights warm, I do not feed the flames as much." I turned to her. "Are you warm?"

"I am, my lord."

"Please call me Geoffrey when we are away from all leaning ears. You have known me longer than anyone in Windsor Castle . . . in this land." She smiled and drank down the wine. "More?"

She held her cup for me to fill again.

"How is my son fairing?"

"He is well cared for, my . . . Geoffrey. He is in good health and most alert for his age."

"Is he back with the nursemaid?"

"Another of the same." She reached out and touched my arm. "He is in good care, Geoffrey. Do not fret."

I smiled and tossed back my wine.

"Tell me, then, beautiful Adelaide, how did you come to be a lady-in-waiting when born into nobility?"

"'Tis a long sad tale, but a swift reply will suffice. My father was purse keeper for all of Anjou."

"I remember."

"Some high nobles accused him of keeping more than his share of accounts and deprived him of his title and all land and property. My father assured me a fraudulent monk was to blame, but 'tis my father was exiled. My mother died, and I gathered what I could and fled. I attended kind nobles in Rouen until Queen Adeliza discovered me while she traveled and asked to have me attend her. I am indeed fortunate she brought me with her to Windsor Castle." She looked sad but proud. "I will bore you not with more."

I touched her hand with mine. "You are still noble, fair Adelaide, and you will remain so with me. Your misfortune will not last. You are the fairest in all the realm."

She blushed and I eased closer, holding onto her hand until our eyes met again, and I leaned in to kiss her soft lips. She pressed mine harder and we embraced, both of us longing for much more as I let slip the scarlet belt from her gown.

13

One warm day, Godfrei found me. "Sir Geoffrey, the king has returned from his hunting and wishes to see you."

"Where is King Henry, Godfrei?"

"He visited Lady Matilda and your son and has retreated to the chapel, my lord. Join him there." He dipped his head and departed.

I rose from the chessboard and eyed my opponent across the table. "We shall finish this, Hardouin," I said to my military advisor.

"When I shall cry 'victory,' my lord."

I laughed and walked to the chapel in hopes of good tidings. Standing at the back, I waited as the kneeling king heaved himself up from the altar and cleared my throat.

"Your Grace!"

The king looked about. "Come, Geoffrey, I must speak to you while my men attend to the meat on this heated day. We must not have it spoil."

"A good hunt, King Henry?"

"Indeed. 'Tis been a long while since a respectable hunt. We took greyhounds and watched them overrun wild game. My new mount did his best as well."

"I am pleased to hear this. What game did you bring back?"

"A fine boar and two foxes for fur. My own arrow missed a generous hart but my men brought it down. They are unmaking it for the evening meal. Fresh venison will be a delight since our stores after the harsh winter have not yet been filled to capacity."

"Even royal pottage became hard to swallow although we were blessed to have it when many had nought to eat."

"Ah," the king said, motioning me closer as he sat down near the altar. "Geoffrey, I have visited Matilda and the babe. He is an exceptional one and will no doubt make a worthy king one day."

"I agree, sire."

"I now implore you to spill fertile seed for another heir."

Bile rose in my throat. "So soon, Your Grace?"

"Do not question me, Sir Geoffrey! The world is a cruel and dangerous place, and one heir—while he is perfect now—is not sufficient. I must have more heirs in the event a horror befalls him in health or injury. Do you not agree?" His eyes bore into mine.

I swallowed hard. While I had no desire to agree, I knew the king was accurate in his assessment and that he would take no less than accord on my part. I nodded without words, fretful of more unwanted intimacy with Matilda.

"I want more enthusiasm from both you and Matilda!"

"Your Grace—"

"Nought that you say will sway me!" he bellowed with a red face. I closed my mouth. "Now go and see to your assignment." He dismissed me with a flick of his hand.

Rutting with a shrew was the last task I wanted, but I promised King Henry heirs when I married his daughter. Dread invaded my heart as I hung my head and left the disgruntled king alone in the chapel.

Familiar anxieties swept over me as I entered my lady wife's chamber.

"I am more vexed than you, Geoffrey, but we must procreate," Matilda said before I had spoken a word. I looked at gray cold stone walls that resembled my feelings for my lady wife. The thought of coupling in her bed made me ill.

"'Tis soon."

"I am healed from Henry's birth, my husband. I will prepare for nightfall," she said, dismissing me with rancor.

✣ ✣ ✣

At the evening meal, Matilda drank heavily and her giddiness followed us to the bedchamber and made my required entrance more tolerable for both of us, although we performed dispassionately.

Fortnights passed at slug pace, Matilda only able to endure my presence when slopped with wine.

"Mayhap our fruitfulness will present another heir with dispatch," she said after a bout in bed while I prayed diligently for my seed to flow swiftly to its target.

"Open the gates! Stephen of Blois, Count of Mortain, nephew of the king, approaches," the sentry called out.

All knights in the courtyard turned as the chatelaine barked orders to the wait-staff. The king appeared at an upper balcony and stayed there until Stephen and his men rode their mounts across the bridge and dismounted, giving their reins to squires who had scrambled from the castle stables. The king motioned for his nephew to be escorted up to him as we knights entertained his five men. Thirsts were quenched and bellies filled as the men became rowdy and began to move about the castle as if they belonged there.

I spied one soldier chasing a maiden into a dark corner, but before I could move in her direction, Blou came up beside me, a grim look on his face.

"I like this not," he whispered near my ear, gritting his teeth. "They show no manners, my lord."

"None," I answered with caution. "Be ever diligent in watch, Blou." I sensed all was not well. Mayhap the nephew brought mischief and mayhem with him, but I said nought. Stephen of Blois was the son of King Henry's older deceased brother and word was he should rightfully become king once Henry died. The king's lone son and true male heir had died, leaving his daughter—my lady wife—his sole heir. But we all knew countless high nobles were against Matilda— or any female—ascending the throne. I gripped the hilt of my dagger, my head and heart ready to do battle if the enemy was within easy reach and a threat to my young son or his legacy.

The night was uneasy with unwelcomed guests, but sleep overtook me and wrapped me in a tight web until I heard a scream and footfalls on the hall stone. I sluggishly grabbed my sword and opened my chamber door, just in time to see Stephen chasing Adelaide around the far corner. I followed in pursuit and found Stephen just as he slammed my mistress's back into a stone wall and rucked up her chemise. I stuck the point of my blade into his back and he froze, Adelaide breathing hard with wild eyes set on me.

"Release her!" I bellowed, sticking the blade deep enough to draw blood. Stephen let Adelaide go and she ran away as he turned towards me with a nasty sneer on his face.

"Just a little evening's entertainment, my good man," he uttered. "No need have you to pierce me. Your hospitality leaves much to be desired, Geoffrey Plantagenet." He stepped in my direction.

"Proceed no further or my blade will penetrate your foolishness."

I gritted my teeth and put my blade under his arrogant chin, backing him down the long corridor and around the corner to the outside door. I continued to move him backwards to the castle gate.

"Lower the bridge!" I yelled to the sentry, who scrambled up from a deep sleep and stared down at me. "Lower it now, I say!"

The sentry did as I commanded and I prodded the unwelcomed guest across the moat and away from the castle.

"My men! My horse!" Stephen cried out when he saw that I was furious and unrelenting.

"They will follow," I told him. "You are not welcome here. Do not return!"

I shoved him and ran back across the bridge, signaling the sentry to raise it. After rousing the others of his band and their horses, the bridge lowered long enough to send them forth, grumbling and waving angry fists as they went, many of them not wearing so much as a dagger. I cared not where they went or how they fared. I looked up at the king, who remained at his balcony but said nought. I walked the long hall towards the queen mother's chamber but stopped when I heard whimpering behind a nearby curtain. I pulled it back to find Adelaide cowering there on the stone floor. I took her in my arms.

"Did he harm you?"

"No, my lord." She dipped her head. "I was on errand from Queen Adeliza who is deprived of rest." She looked relieved and grateful, wiping her eyes. "I must get back to her."

I released her even though I wanted to embrace her until she ceased to tremble in the sunrise of the morrow.

✠ ✠ ✠

Matilda laid calculating eyes on me when I visited the next morn. "What of the night's ruckus?"

"Your cousin, Stephen, attempted to have his way with the queen mother's attendant."

"Ah, and you saved the maiden from foul harm," she blurted.

"Your cousin is indeed foul."

"I must speak to my father about his visit here. I know not if he sent for Stephen or if he came on his own. I do not trust Stephen. He wants the throne and will do whatever is necessary to attain it. I was not summoned to their talks. 'Tis distressing to me."

"Nor did the king summon me. The castle has been uneasy since your cousin's arrival, his men rowdy and ill-mannered, but he and his men are gone. I told them never to return."

She nodded her appreciation. "'Tis time for my father to make good on his promises to me and make known his wishes for me to follow him to the throne. I will ask you to join me when I speak with him."

"As you wish, my lady wife." I bowed and made ready to leave.

"I *know*, Geoffrey."

"Pardon?"

She thrust her chin out and up. "I know of your dalliance with the queen's maiden. Or shall I call her a courtesan?"

"Dare *not*! Lady Adelaide and I have known each other since we played in my father's courtyard as children," I responded.

"And you *still* play!"

I walked back to her. "I confess it," I said holding my head high. "I love her. She is a gentle, kind spirit and comes from nobility."

"But she is no longer noble."

"I have no doubt she will once again belong to nobility."

"How, with you taking her for a mistress?"

"Matilda, what concerns you? You oft times turn away my advances. You embarrass and humiliate me at every turn. You make clear that you feel nought but loathing for me." My voice grew louder as I stepped close enough to bite her long maligning nose. "Our distrust for one another grows stronger each day."

"'Mayhap, but you must show discretion in matters of such a sensitive nature." She clucked her tongue like a hen.

"I do."

She scoffed. "I do not care for this arrangement, but if you do love her, I will tolerate it."

"Am I to be grateful for that?"

She whirled and walked away from me. "I care not for your gratitude, Geoffrey. I simply remind you these walls have curtains behind which ears and eyes pry. Watch yourself. Humiliate me not!"

✛ ✛ ✛

"I wish to be away . . . away from these dark cold walls," Matilda declared after one evening. I blinked. "And from you and your court . . . your mistress."

"The weather is warm. Open your windows or walk outside," I said. She remained silent. "Where will you go? Who goes with you for your protection? After all, you are the king's heir. Some would welcome a chance to do you harm to prevent such an ascension."

"Your concern is touching, Geoffrey, but I will not be alone." Her voice was clipped.

"Does Richard of York come for you here?" Her head shot up. "I know, Matilda. One only has to observe his manner when in your presence."

She smiled. "He comes for me, but we are befriended and nothing more."

"Then you use him to your own cause." I sighed loudly and shook my head.

"And what of young Henry?"

"He remains here."

"You would leave your child to travel far?"

"He has nursemaids who chase after his swift legs now. Their care far exceeds my own," she admitted.

Her words were true. "Go then!" I yelled in her face. "I will gladly attend to my son!"

"And if you are called to war in a far land?"

"Lady Adelaide will—"

"Lady Adelaide is here to attend Queen Adeliza."

"She is adept at both. And the queen should spend time with Henry so that he has some remembrance of her."

Matilda dipped her head and nodded. "I must see to my trunk. A hansom and brougham will transport me."

"Then I will hinder you no longer. I trust you will entertain your own company more than mine." I started away but looked around at her. "Remember, Matilda, you take your true self with you wherever you roam."

Her back stiffened but she uttered not a word.

✤ ✤ ✤

Fishing proved worthy during summer days when heat kept us near cool rivers. Some days I took young Henry and we splashed about for hours. I never tired of his laughter, his energy, and his generous affection towards me. I thanked God for him in my life.

"Fi," my son managed, pointing into the water.

"Fish," I repeated for him.

He splashed water with the palm of his hands, delighted at the noise and spray he made. I giggled with him and splashed back gently before I picked him up and planted a kiss on his rosy cheek. He filled my heart with love in daylight and Adelaide fulfilled my unrestrained desires during darkness, both of us with rasping breaths, our bodies trembling in ecstasy. I had never known such contentment.

✤ ✤ ✤

One day towards summer's end, my squire and I tethered our horses near the forest and pulled in a good day's catch before lazing in the shade of a river oak while a slight breeze rustled just enough to help us doze. When Count whinnied, I bolted up, dagger drawn. A startled doe hastened away from us, her white tail high behind her.

"Do we give chase, m'lord?"

"She is more than a bow shot away and the mounts would be hard pressed to catch that one, Frick." We watched the doe disappear into the far western forest. I sat there looking over the vast property owned by King Henry.

"Mount up, Frick. I wish you to see a special place."

We let the horses trot in the heat, crossed the field, and dismounted where land rose in front of us.

"Tether the mounts here, Frick." He did as I asked and we walked together up the highest hill on the king's land. At its zenith we could view the expanse of the kingdom in every direction.

"Remember this place, my squire. If the enemy approaches and battle looms, you may be ordered here to scout and report back to knights in the castle or in the field behind us."

"I will remember." We took in the beauty of plush crops and fields, the swift waters moving downstream, and mountain peaks to the northwest.

"Let us descend and mount up."

The horses had rested, so I slapped Count's flank and he galloped. "Keep up, Frick," I yelled over my shoulder. Nutmeg soon galloped beside my mount and we held up in the apple orchard where we feasted on sweet juicy treats along with Count and Nutmeg. I bagged apples to take back to the castle.

"We shall have fish and fruit to eat, my squire."

When we returned, I saw the hansom and brougham, surprised my lady wife had returned unannounced. When I entered the corridor, young Henry toddled to me, reddish gold hair he inherited from me in disarray.

"He rested well," the nursemaid told me with a smile.

I looked about.

"Lady Matilda has returned, Sir Geoffrey," she added.

"Where?"

"She is in her private chamber, but she wishes not to be disturbed, my lord."

I cared not what she wished. I pushed past the nursemaid and stomped into the room.

"You intrude!" Matilda roared at me, her eyes wet and red.

"I see a holiday improved not your disposition," I shot back at her.

She lowered herself to the chaise, covered her face and wept. I had never seen her cry.

"What is amiss?"

"I should never have gone, Geoffrey."

"What troubles you, Matilda?"

"What troubles me? You yourself said it: where ere I roam I take myself with me. I do not care for myself as I have been to you. I have let pride, vanity and entitlement come between us. You never had a chance to know the good in me."

I clamped my lips to keep my tongue quiet and poured us each a cup of wine. She took the cup and swallowed its contents while I sipped mine.

"Can you forgive me, Geoffrey?"

"We are both to blame, Matilda, but more so the circumstances of our union. 'Twas a political alliance made in haste with no time for true affection to grow. We have had this talk many times. Nothing has changed."

"We are older and wiser. Mayhap we can now forge our own alliance for the sake of our heirs."

"Heirs?"

"I am again with child."

I backed away from her. "Am I the father or is Richard?"

"*You* are the father, Geoffrey! Trust me. Richard, it seems, prefers a hairy chest and a steel dagger that can thrust from behind!"

14

After Matilda's stunning announcements, I relieved tension to some degree by carrying out my daily routine until King Henry summoned me again to his chamber.

"Troubling news arrived that dissent among barons and nobles in Anjou grows strong once more." He stared at me. "You are to send a man—Hardouin, your military adviser— to survey the depths of this revolt."

After a lengthy session on matters of state, I summoned Hardouin and got him on his way. I then called for my squire.

"You sent for me, m'lord?"

"Frick, we will be called to Anjou anon. I have sent Hardouin, who will return and advise us. Prepare all manner of supplies with Paieri's help and plan to ride with us when the time comes."

My squire jumped about and waved his arms with excitement.

"These are dangerous times." I took his shoulders in my hands and looked him in the eye. "'Tis *not* a game we play now. 'Tis not practice."

"I am ready, m'lord." He blinked at me. "And I have built a siege weapon for that purpose."

"A weapon?"

"The smith helped me with the metal. Come, I will show you."

I laid down my sword and walked with Frick to the shelter behind the stables where he yanked a cloth from a device like none I had seen before. I studied it. "An onager of some sort?"

"Aye, m'lord. Let me demonstrate."

We pulled the device out into open field and turned it away from the stables and livery.

"I have gathered stones when I could," Frick said, running to retrieve a heavy sack.

Two beams of sturdy oak made up the framework. I watched as my squire twisted rope around a spoke and loaded a stone. He forced the spoke down and released it, hurling the projectile far into the meadow.

"I have heard of siege weapons but have never had the use of one. You are, indeed, a talented lad, Leofrick. I shall call you a master artilleryman."

"I am pleased, m'lord. Can we take it to battle?"

"I think not." He hid not his disappointment. "It would slow us. Let it remain here at the castle to offer the king, queen and future heirs security if an enemy approaches." He beamed with pride. "You continue to amaze me. From whence come your many talents?"

"I know not, m'lord."

"'Tis to lofty military heights you shall rise one day, my squire."

The grin he wore was soon on my face besides.

Dissent had also reached the palace, with relations between King Henry, Matilda and I strained. Even so my lady wife and I met with the king over the dowry dispute to assure us a more powerful position. In the end, King Henry granted her various Norman castles, but he enlightened us not on when she could take possession of them. I sensed he used shrewdness in the matter mayhap fearing I would overstep my bounds as her husband. However, the king did summons English nobles to council where they gave an oath of allegiance to Matilda as the king's heir apparent. Even with this oath, Matilda and I felt a lack of genuine support in England and met again with the king to ask him to hand over the royal castles in Normandy to Matilda anon and implore Norman nobility to swear allegiance to her as well.

"I will not!" The king bellowed and his face reddened. "'Tis *you*, Sir Geoffrey Plantagenet, who would seize power in Normandy!" He pointed a pudgy finger at me.

"Your Grace, Matilda and I have presented you with an heir and another to come. I am about preserving a place for them, a kingdom and one day the throne for Henry there." Holding my own temper proved a difficult task.

"I will hear no more words this night," King Henry said. He dismissed both of us with the flip of his wrist.

The royal refusal to hand over the dowry I had been promised when I married Matilda was a punch in my face. His mounting antagonism puzzled me. I only knew the relationship between us would deteriorate further.

My demeanor worsened, for the king had not encouraged my ruling England and Normandy at my lady wife's side. He had not granted me Anglo-Norman lands, nor had he invited me to attend court since my marriage to his daughter. I was neither allowed to stand beside Matilda as she received oaths from magnates. My patience had run its course and my temper had taken control, making me hostile at every turn. King Henry seemed to have no intention of ceding control of border castles even though they were promised. The king and I did not speak for months on end. Though Matilda sided with me on the issue, both of us feared our son's future claims could be compromised at any moment.

The approach of winter sequestered us inside. I attended to knightly duties and matters of the crown, concerned the castle and all therein—particularly my lady wife and son— were in vulnerable circumstances. One evening Matilda, bundled and near the fire's embers, gestured for me to sit near her.

"You must eat more, Matilda. You need strength for all that is ahead of us."

"I know what to expect, Geoffrey. I have given birth prior." Her sour tone irked me further.

"No, not only the forthcoming birth. I fear King Henry's refusal to give us the promised dowry leaves your legacy in jeopardy. Norman castles should now be in our hands with England's to follow upon your father's death."

"He wants me to take the throne, Geoffrey. Of that I have no doubt but I must convince him to keep his promise with haste." She rubbed her belly. "I will deliver as spring brings warmth and blooms and then I will take the matter to him once again. Concern yourself not." she said with uplifted head.

"You are pale of face," I said.

"I do not feel well, but that is part of the curse of bearing a child. Don't fret. I will make preparations in the near future." She lapsed into silence as I stayed seated near her. She lifted her head and looked me in the eye.

"Have you heard that the courtesan is no more?" Her eyes bored through mine.

My heart flipped over itself. "The courtesan?"

"Your courtesan, Annique. Your gift for last Feast. Have you forgotten her so soon?"

"Annique?"

"She was found frozen in the first snow, far away between two hamlets. Alone."

I staggered up and felt pain enter my heart, attempting to rein in my outward emotions. Matilda walked to me.

"My husband, it grieves me to see you hurt, but—"

"Bah!" I grabbed her by the shoulders. "You hurt me daily! You promote only discord. You say these words to inflict more pain!"

"That is not so!" She acted as though I had hurt *her*. "I merely thought you cared enough to hear of her pitiful demise."

I could not cast my watery eyes towards Matilda who continued, her voice soft and sweet with a compassion I knew she did not own. "She taught you well, Geoffrey. I am forever grateful."

I lifted my head, saying nought before I left the chamber, closing the big heavy door softly behind me.

Sadness surrounded my heart, my private time spent recalling my first uneasy encounter with Annique, subsequent training lessons and our last tryst in my bath during the Feast of Saint Nicholas nearly a year prior. I had not seen her since that night. I had saved a ribbon and bead from her wimple and took them out now and rubbed them in my hands before I hurled the keepsakes into the hearth's flames and prayed for her soul. That she had died a slow death alone rent my heart in two.

On the morrow, I met my lady wife halfway down the corridor, her attendants struggling to hold her up.

"What is amiss?"

"The baby is coming," one attendant announced.

Matilda doubled over. "Ah! The wretched pain!" Her face reddened and she started to slide towards the floor.

I scooped her into my arms, walked swiftly to her bedchamber, and gently placed her in the bed as the physician rushed in.

"'Tis not yet time," he said with concern. He disappeared into the chamber to examine her and stepped out to tell me the baby would be born later in the day—ready or not— thus I headed towards my chamber to bathe and await the birth. I turned the corner and began the long walk.

"Sir Geoffrey!"

I turned to see the beatific face of Adelaide at the hall intersect as she walked towards me. I opened my chamber door, urged her inside, and closed the door. She kissed me with great affection but I did not reciprocate.

"What troubles you, Geoffrey?"

"My lady wife is in labor and 'tis not yet time for the birth."

"Oh," she said as she put distance between us. "I hope all goes well for both Lady Matilda and the baby."

I noticed she trembled. "Are you cold?"

"I am," she replied, moving towards the warmth of the hearth. She turned to the side and I stared at her silhouette, shocked at what I saw there.

"Adelaide?"

She dropped her head. "I am with child, Geoffrey. *Your* child. No other has touched me."

Her lips parted as I approached and touched first her belly and then her face, pulling it to my lips. Our eyes never wavered from one another. As much as I longed to hold Adelaide and celebrate this moment, I assured her of my devotion and sent her away so I could bathe and attend to a more pressing matter.

❖ ❖ ❖

I sat on the cold stone floor outside Matilda's bedchamber. I listened to cries of anguish from her all afternoon and into darkness until I heard the infant's ragged cry and rested back, thinking of all the challenges I now faced in my personal life.

After more time, the physician came out but blocked my entrance. "I am distressed, Sir Geoffrey. The baby is small and in a fragile state. Lady Matilda is in dreadful condition."

I looked past him, hoping to see into the room. "Please, I want to see them."

"I will let you pass, but remember they are weak and exhausted after all the hours of labor to get him here. Pray they both survive, Sir Geoffrey."

I stepped in and went first to my lady wife, ashen and it seemed barely breathing. Ladies all around her bed attended her, one wiping her brow with cold cloths. I heard no cries from the baby and went in search of him. I found him being tended by the physician's nursemaids adjacent to Matilda's chamber.

"Is he breathing?"

"He is, my lord, yet he is exhausted from his journey. We will nourish him to good health," Guinevere whispered to me with a faint smile. "I fear he fares better than his mother, Sir Geoffrey."

I heard the crier announcing the baby's birth outside the castle and bells clanged, but I stayed back from the balcony, more concerned with my lady wife and son.

"Where is Henry?" I asked.

She motioned towards the adjoining chamber. "He was removed to another chamber farther from his mother's cries, Sir Geoffrey, but he returns to the nursery now."

I nodded and walked back by Matilda's bed where I was hard pressed to recognize her. One of her attendants pulled the feather coverlet up to her damp shoulders.

I nodded and walked to the adjoining chamber to see the infant now swaddled and warm in his cradle. Young Henry looked over the cradle with curiosity but when he saw me he ran to me, his arms outstretched. I whisked him from the floor, kissing his cheeks and then his chubby fingers. He smiled up at me with an adoration I found nowhere else.

"You have a brother, young Henry," I announced to him. I walked to the cradle and we both looked down at the tiny baby.

"Henry's hair, like yours, is the color of an evening sunset." I looked over my shoulder at Adelaide.

"You are tending them?"

"'Til Marie arrives," she replied, looking down. "She attends your lady wife."

I studied her, noticing how pale her skin had become. "Are you ailing?"

"No, I am fine." She turned her eyes from mine. In a whisper, she continued. "But I fear I should leave here, Geoffrey. 'Tis unbecoming to be under the same roof with your lady wife and the heirs . . . your sons." I stared and blinked a few times, comprehending her words. "Queen Adeliza is advising me and contemplates my dilemma."

"No!" I yelled, scaring Henry and tiny Geoffrey, who wailed and sent Adelaide scurrying to them. I got control of my voice and whispered, "I will not have you leave after we have found one another again."

She gathered Geoffrey in one arm and calmed Henry with the other.

"You will be a fine mother, Adelaide, but I want you here with my sons . . . with *me*."

"'Tis out of my control, Geoffrey. I would never have been hence if I had not found favor with Queen Adeliza. I dare not betray her if she wants to send me away. Scandal is unwanted."

"'Tis not out of *my* control," I said at the threshold between the rooms.

I tapped on the queen's door and an attendant led me to her, sitting by the hearth, bundled as though she were out in the cold weather. Her griffon, Gristle, got up and ambled over to sniff me.

"Geoffrey, I have heard of my grandson's arrival. I am pleased he is here even though his early arrival raised concern."

"Much concern remains," I said.

"I heard." She patted the ottoman beside her. "Come and sit by the fire," she invited cordially.

"I am warm enough, Queen Adeliza," I nodded, standing still a distance from her. "I came to beseech you not to remove your attendant from the castle."

"You have spoken with Lady Adelaide then." She shifted a bit under heavy wraps. "I am most distressed, Geoffrey. She carries your bastard under the same roof as your true sons and heirs. Could you not have had a discreet dalliance away from the castle?"

"You know that she is with child?"

"I do. She confides much in me as I do her. I, of course, had noticed her growing belly as others surely will."

The queen rose and faced me. "If Lady Adelaide stays nearby, you must refrain from contact with her, or at least use discretion. There will be a multitude of whispers and questions as she swells and gives birth. I adore her, Geoffrey, and wish not to have her disgraced. I will make my own decision and tell no one of the child's father," she said to me in a whisper. "You will have more than your share to worry about with your lady wife."

I nodded, and as she dismissed me, Gristle cocked his leg and relieved himself on my boot, adding insult to injury. I hung my head slightly and backed out of the room, my heart heavily burdened.

✣ ✣ ✣

After sending my pissed boots with Godfroi, I walked to the nursery where young Henry and I spent the night together. I held him in my arms as he slept a peaceful sleep and I prayed.

Matilda worsened over the sinnight but roused enough to make her final wishes known. She and her physician thought the end neared. I paced the halls and rooms, a helpless knight . . . husband . . . under such circumstance. Nought I had learned in my adult life had taught me how to deal with such matters as sickness and death. Clergy of the highest order were all around, so I left Matilda's fate in their hands and worried about our infant son instead.

With prayers from all over the realm, Matilda's health improved daily and she honored me by naming our second son Geoffrey.

In a still weak voice she proclaimed, "You have displayed great bravery and skill in military conflicts for the sake of the kingdom and its rightful heirs, my husband. Even though he lacks strength now, your namesake shall do likewise."

15

Peace allowed the household to meld into a comfortable and amicable routine even though news from abroad was worrisome. Matilda healed and our private times were less stressful for both of us. I had never before witnessed a weak and fragile lady wife so I was shocked at how close Death had come to claiming her. The experience seemed to have an effect on her demeanor as well. She no longer spewed hostile words at me. Although I seldom bedded her, I studied her now, dressed in a stunning gown and glowing with makeup.

"Your health and strength appear improved," I said the morning after a pleasant night together.

"Indeed. I tire of the sick bed and its chamber and wish to dress elegantly and walk about. I may ride in the pasture later."

"I am pleased to hear of it. You will soon ride full pelt."

She smiled and joined me to break fast. On our walk to the Great Hall, I told her a bawdy joke and we both laughed. It occurred to me that it was perchance the first time we had laughed together in all the years of our marriage.

Our second son grew stronger by the day under the physician's guidance and much monitoring and endearment from Matilda's ladies-in-waiting. The dowager had, indeed, sent Adelaide away to Carrington Nunnery attached to the

Church of Saint Mary in Somerset to have the baby and I
pleaded with her to have her return with the child—my
child—in her arms. My plea had not yet been answered and
I was not allowed to visit.

In the meantime, Roger of Salisbury rode in late one
evening and dined with the king in privacy. I was then
summoned.

"A fresh rebellion erupts in Normandy," the king
announced on a sunny day. "'Tis become more a revolution.
Roger tells me his very life has been in jeopardy over
accounts and greed. I tire of this constant annoyance." His
eyes met mine. "Let us swiftly there and quell discontent,
Geoffrey."

This would be my first highly-anticipated military
campaign with King Henry, who hoped his mere presence
in the discontented country would end dispute without war.
My heart raced and I hoped to do battle but have no blood
spilt from our own train.

The king and his entourage along with a liege army of
knights, squires and marshals rode east as one and reached
the channel. The king and his attendants crossed in his
dragon-headed long ship while we crossed in another long
ship behind him. Blou, Hardouin and I planned maneuvers
as we crossed. Once we made landfall with well-fed men
and rested mounts, we galloped south, thundering past fields
and through hamlets near our path.

King Henry campaigned with his military household,
united barons and nobility, not willing to hear more from
the Duke of Normandy himself or any of his party.

"Arm yourselves!" The king bellowed. "The enemy will
only listen to the hiss of arrows!" We knelt in prayer before
we wiped down our swords and filled our quivers.

I looked over at Frick. "I knew not I brought you to
fierce combat."

"Fear not, Sir Geoffrey, I am ready."

I nodded and tried to hide my apprehension.

"God ride with us," the king declared as we mounted and he took the lead. Jaquelin stayed behind at camp. King Henry instructed us to apprehend William, Count of Ponthieu, leader of the revolt, by any means possible. I remembered the count and his disrespect from my last encounter, and relished the man's undoing by my own hand.

❖ ❖ ❖

Steel flashed. Sparks flew from swords to helmets and other swords. Screams resonated across fields and over hills in all directions where men fought. I became stronger upon the flanks of Honor whose strength I could feel as we moved forward. Fighting on the wide beast added strength and power to my spear, the iron tip penetrating all wood, leather or bone it encountered. Mounts slammed into one another but Honor never lost footing. Axe fighting maimed many and I endured bruises and cuts. Honor stood steadfast, a true warrior himself. We battled 'til all the earth shook. Men died by sword or by trampling under horse hoofs. Some of our foes became our captives with much relief on their faces. My armor, gouged in many places, saved me from injury.

A messenger searched me out to whisper that my lady wife had formed an army in Normandy against her own father, with my knowledge but not his. To ensure word spread no further, I sent the messenger swiftly to England to report back on my family there.

Our train forded a river and headed east. We knew our stout mounts could not maneuver the thickness of the forest. Taking a longer route cost us a day's journey but when our army emerged from an outcropping of rock in full warfare, the enemy at first appeared quietened. Nevertheless, the king ordered us to set upon them, ready to end repeated dissension in his own kingdom once and for all time. Horses galloped, men shouted, arrows whirred on both sides of the fray.

Once we had driven deep into enemy lines, I pulled my sword and dismounted. I slashed, thrust, and plunged as arrows whirred by my helmet, moving with great dexterity and unspoken apprehension that became a rush of exhilarated madness until Hardouin grabbed my shoulders and pulled me backwards.

"Geoffrey! You have beaten the poor man senseless! He surrendered."

I looked down at the bloodied man who held up a trembling hand to me before he fell over with a thud. I remembered his face from childhood. I had played in forests and fields with him, but did not remember his name. I stared down at what I had done. His right ear dangled and his matted hair bled down his whimpering face. With shame, I turned away.

From where had all the force and anger in my body come?

I attacked men here—some of them former friends— fueled by my frustrations with Matilda, my discontent with King Henry and my longing for Adelaide. I ended my violent attack, backing farther away with disbelief.

"You are injured, Sir Geoffrey," Frick called out. I had noticed not my injuries, only those I had inflicted on others.

Twilight came as enraged clouds gathered over us. We pulled back our warriors and surveyed gory fields. The day's toll lay before us in human butchery. Covered in blood, sweat, and filth, we returned to camp where cooking fires burned and aromas of many kinds drifted into our path. As hungry as I was, my appetite abandoned me. My thoughts on all the carnage left on the battlefields of my homeland rendered me off-color.

"My lord, you must eat for strength. The battle renews on the morrow." Jacquelin offered me a loaf and a cup.

"Not now."

"While 'tis warm, my lord Geoffrey."

I sighed and took food to the kitchener's satisfaction, finishing it just as King Henry summoned me to his private tent. With a heavy sigh, I walked to the king's tent flap and entered.

"This finishes on the morrow, Geoffrey," he said emphatically. "I and my men will turn back to the north to hunt while you bring victory back to England. 'Twill be a feather in your cap . . . or mayhap you prefer a sprig of broom." He shifted his heft and looked at me. I feigned a weak smile. "Your physical presence, military tactics and leadership have made a favorable impression. Your youth is no more. It has vanished and left in its place a splendid warrior due all respect."

"But my heart is heavy, Your Grace," I confessed. "As a child I played games with many of these men."

"'Tis true that battle brings bloodshed and ends friendships, Geoffrey, but our enemy here had only to concede to prevent such slaughter."

I could form no words of disagreement so I took my leave. "I wish you safe travel, Your Grace. We will—" Thunder boomed and the night sky lit with fire, followed by a torrent of rain.

King Henry shrugged his shoulders. "Mayhap we will delay our journey hence." We said our parting words and I ran to my own tent. After rainfall became heavier and lightning bolder, I shot out of my tent and ran into the field behind our camp. I threw my arms into the air and dared lightning to strike me down. I turned in every direction, providing an open target until I began to cry and plowed into a miserable heap in mud.

I know not how long I stayed there but when I came to my senses, I walked into a nearby stream and bathed blood and the smell of death from my body. Then I hunkered down in my tent without speaking a word to anyone. A plan of attack for the morrow had been made over the evening meal with my military adviser, Hardouin, in charge.

✤ ✤ ✤

Winds howled and rains kept us in our tents, the campfires drenched. My own candle flickered while rain drummed the canvas. I blew it out and at last welcomed sleep. I knew the enemy could not find us and attack in such abominable weather.

Later a strong arm rustled me awake. "My lord?"

"Hardouin?"

"Sir Geoffrey, rain has ceased. Do we keep with our plan?"

I scrambled up. In darkness before dawn we broke fast, equipped ourselves with leather, mail, helmets and steel. Mounted, I bowed my head towards the king, peering out at us from inside his tent as I passed him, and led my men stealthily towards our unsuspecting targets. We urged our horses forward with quietness through the undulating countryside I knew so well, its autumn hues wet and flattened by downpours. Dawn chased us, its light becoming stronger behind us.

Near the enemy's camp we quietly aligned ourselves, drew our swords and thundered into their encampment. We caught our foe in slumber and overran tents. We turned our mounts and stormed back as frightened men appeared from under their flattened lodging with weapons drawn. Their pickets of horses were out of reach. They fought us on foot with no armor or helmets in a swift and deadly massacre I would never forget. Our bodies collided, swords drawn, swinging, making contact, and ducking to avoid injury ourselves. Axes hit their marks, blood spurted, and men let go primal screams. Adrenaline controlled my body, no longer my own but part of something bigger and stronger than myself. When bone fragments hit my helmet, adrenaline left me as swiftly as it had begun.

Our enemies who were able, fled on foot. Those who stood fast paid a high cost. The roar of battle drowned my orders and I yelled again at full volume. "Hold! Hold, I say!"

My men at first stared at me and then rearranged themselves near me.

I looked about me into astounded faces, bloody and covered with mud. I turned my eyes away from the horror and wept openly on my knees. Blou touched my shaking shoulder. "We will see to the dead and injured captives, my lord." I could not so much as nod. I stared in a stupor as men with cattle carts rounded the field to collect corpses of men I knew slain this very day, many at my own hand.

Horses had thrown their riders and with broken reins they wandered about whinnying as if in shock.

Back at our camp, a victory celebration ensued in which I took no part.

"I was no true warrior this day, but instead a butcher," I muttered aloud, my voice trembling. I slammed my hand into the table board and took to my tent in agonizing reflection over the day's events. When I emerged, I sat beside Frick—somber, filthy and silent—at the campfire. A bright moon gave us light enough to see all the men and our mounts on pickets. Many eyes set on me but I avoided locking mine on any of them. After a while, Frick dared to look my way.

"What is amiss with the moon's light, m' lord?" I had watched as the full bright moon was covered in darkness and then was likewise uncovered.

"'Tis an eclipse. A sign," I uttered in a low voice.

"What kind of sign, m'lord?"

Before I could answer my squire, Paieri called out, "An omen, lad. Something unsettling will occur. Let us hope it unsettles the enemy and not ourselves."

All the men looked back at the moon, lost in their own private thoughts. I recalled the crone's words: "Dark of moon brings realm of gloom."

What could that mean?

I shook off the apprehension in my chest but slept with my weapons ready beside me for fear a new enemy would ambush us on this perplexing night.

✣ ✣ ✣

Loud hoofs came into camp in the darkness and stopped at my tent. I threw back the tent's flap, my dagger ready to strike the first blow.

"What is amiss, Cai?" I asked, recognizing him from the king's liege.

"'Tis the king, my lord. He is unwell. You must come at once!"

"Paieri, to horse!"

Men in camp scrambled as word spread of the bad tidings.

16

The messenger was provided a fresh mount and he rode with me to Lyons-le-Foret Castle near the king's hunting lodge at Rouen. Mortecai and I rode full pelt, not speaking a word until daybreak when we dismounted to water our mounts.

"A hunting mishap?"

"No, Sir Geoffrey. King Henry dined on an excess of lamprey pie at the lodge and fell ill. The cook said he advised the king against eating the delicacy due to the unfresh smell of the meat, but he gorged himself, eating the whole of it. His condition worsened and I was sent for you."

"He ate the pie in its entirety?"

"Always, Sir Geoffrey." I had to shake my head in disbelief.

We mounted up and trotted down a dirt path near a thick stand of trees. As if the dark and damp coldness were not misery enough, an ominous white fog rolled over us, smelling of fermented brew and rot like I had smelled before. Suddenly fire and crackling filled the sky. No, wait! 'Twas cackling. The hags had returned. We grabbed out sword hilts, ready to strike. One hideous creature came into view and unleashed a horrid noise, pointing her bony tendrilled finger at me.

"Man of broom, dark of moon brings realm of gloom," she cried in a hoarse voice.

"Remember!" a voice shouted, causing Count to back up, stomp and blow.

"Remember!" came another voice from my left side.

"Remember!" they all shouted in unison before the fog cleared and Mortecai and I stared at one another.

"My lord?"

"We must make haste, Cai. I pray the king is not in distress." We spurred our mounts and moved away from the trees.

We rode on and when we arrived, I flung myself from my mount and ran to the king's bedside where earls, counts, and bishops stood with grim faces. Earl William of Warenne was at King Henry's bed and shook his head as I stepped forward to see for myself my father-in-law's condition.

"The king is dead, Sir Geoffrey Plantagenet."

I studied the king's ashen flesh, his last breath gone out of him before my arrival. A candlewick was kindled, blazed up and then extinguished, leaving behind an eerie trail of smoke and solemn silence until Earl William hit a table board with his open palm.

"Those damned foul lampreys!"

We were all startled and stared at the earl and then at the dead monarch.

"King Henry should not have eaten them. They smelled of rot and he still demanded to have them." He let go a heavy sigh. The earl paced up and down the room before he continued. "King Henry honored lowly and great men with his generous spirits, I among them." He turned to others in the room. "He supported us with honors and wealth and was, indeed, just to all subjects." Every man nodded in agreement.

Nicholas of Brighton took the sad news of King Henry's death back to the Palace at Westminster in England. After spending a private moment with King Henry, I again rode full pelt back to my army of men and sent a messenger on from there to deliver the news to Matilda before my arrival.

"Mount up, men!" I shouted to the troops when we were packed. "We must make haste!"

The king's death provided an opportunity to shock southern Normandy and seize key castles—Domfront, Exmes and Argentan—that had formed Matilda's disputed dowry. My men and I met Matilda's loyal army. Joining forces, we took castles with little effort but were then stalled, unable to advance farther as Norman nobility led by William of Ponthieu resisted our advance.

With all claimed castles fortified, I headed back towards Matilda at Argentan, knowing succession to the English throne was now a matter of frantic political speculation. Her pallid countenance brought me up short.

"Geoffrey, I am again with child at a most inopportune time."

I stared at her.

She managed a weak smile. "I am, no doubt, fertile, my husband." She moved with great difficulty to her chaise and eased her body down to it. "I can barely walk. Riding is out of the question."

Therefore, at Argentan, my lady wife was immobilized with her third pregnancy—a surprise to us both—and distraught over her father's death. She was unable to travel back to England for the funeral. She set up household in the four-towered castle and would remain there until our third child was born.

"Sadness fills my very being."

I could hear heartbreak in her voice.

"I must return to Anjou, Matilda. A fresh revolt entangles me and my army and will keep us from crossing the channel to England as well," I said softly.

"I know you must go. I will be here. I pray you hold on to all lands we have laid claim to, Geoffrey. I trust that Henry and Geoffrey are safe with the queen . . . uh, dowager queen now, but I fear our absence will not bode well with my father's court."

"The children are well-protected, I assure you. Rest and be of strong constitution." I hesitated a moment, her eyes coming up to mine before I continued.

"I have heard unsettling news about the castle and I share your worry. I sent out Blou in darkness to see what is amiss and true abroad."

She swung her body awkwardly towards me. "Unsettling news?"

"There is resistance from the nobility in Normandy and England."

"By what cause?"

"A male is expected to take the throne, Matilda. You have known of this desire among nobles. It should come as no surprise."

She threw her nose into the air.

"My father assured me the throne would be *mine*!"

"But, alas, he did nought to assure it with the aristocracy, my lady wife."

She managed to get to her feet, raced to me and grabbed my upper arms. "Stephen! That is why Stephen came to meet with my father. We must stop him, Geoffrey!"

Her face was crimson with anger and worry. I led her back to the chaise, certain my news had upset her even more.

❖ ❖ ❖

By daybreak, word arrived that William of Warenne was escorting the royal corpse to Rouen where King Henry's internal organs would be placed in an urn and buried at

Notre-Dame-de-Pre, the nearby church. His body—filled with aromatic herbs and salt and sewn into layers of ox hide—would lie in state in the abbey church of Saint-Elienne for a fortnight. The remainder of the king's train headed back to England to prepare for a state funeral and the king's interment at Reading Abbey. When the winds of the channel allowed, his body would be taken back to England for burial at the high altar in the Cluniac Abbey at Reading.

I was back in Anjou, detained in a rebellion that never seemed to end. Rumors spread that all of England and Normandy frowned on Matilda's absence from court and nobles looked elsewhere for a new leader. 'Twas rumored the nobles who accompanied Henry's corpse from Rouen went into conclave and proposed the crown go to an alternative candidate, not one bedridden with yet another childbirth. Perchance Matilda was right and decisions about patronage and preferment would favor her upon our return to England. I wondered if Richard of York was behind the unrest and rumors, or mayhap Matilda's ruthless cousin, Stephen. An unshakeable uneasiness crept into my head.

Blou arrived with news from England with staggering body odor.

"Blou, approach not!"

"'Twas sprayed by a foul creature and had no river in which to bathe," he explained.

I waved my hand in front of my nostrils. "Stay at distance and speak your news."

"'Tis unwelcomed news, Sir Geoffrey. Stephen of Mortain moved with great speed to London, where he was welcomed in the absence of Lady Matilda. He then rode seventy miles to Winchester where his youngest brother, Henry, is a bishop. Stephen took the royal treasury and was crowned King of England by the Archbishop of Canterbury."

"Curses! My great fear has been realized," I said.

A decade older than Matilda, Stephen had made his career at the king's court. His Uncle Henry had favored him with the Norman county of Mortain and valued lands in England. High-spirited and effective as a soldier, he remained courteous under normal circumstances. However, neither Matilda nor I thought *this* action courteous. While Matilda's condition compromised travel, she had expected nobles who swore loyalty to protect and hold the monarchy for her.

I slumped. "Blou, I need you here to help with the revolt. I will send Mortecai to keep us informed. Bathe well, fill your belly, and get a fresh horse."

He bowed and headed to the kitchen.

Alas, while I had been entangled in annoying upheaval and Matilda was stranded, Stephen pounced upon the opportunity to offer decisive leadership when England and Normandy teetered on the edge of chaos. Someone would take King Henry's place, so at least Stephen—his nephew—ended the threat of an outsider usurping the throne but his actions did not bode well with me. Matilda and I considered *Stephen* the usurper. Two royal legitimacies now opposed one another and only all-out war could reconcile the dispute.

Matilda, weighed down with child, could do nothing to help herself. My constant entanglement in Anjou had grown exasperating but I dared not leave the duchy or face losing all ground I had gained. Normandy had nearly disintegrated into chaos since the king's death. With the channel separating me from England, I focused all my attention on defeating belligerent Norman landowners and launched an onslaught of vicious raids while I waited for more news.

✣ ✣ ✣

Charles of Toulouse arrived with a message a sinnight later. "My Lord Geoffrey, King David of Scotland tried to assist your lady wife's cause."

"By what means?"

"King David, inflamed with a zeal for justice, pretended to pay the new king a visit but instead marched to Carlisle and Newcastle and captured both. He then called his people to arms and let loose a fierce battle on the English people who disregarded Lady Matilda's right."

"May he be blessed," I responded.

"But, alas, Sir Geoffrey, King Stephen assembled a great and swift army and led it against King David, who had to surrender but would not swear fealty to anyone but his niece."

"Bad news then follows good," I whispered.

"Aye, my lord. When King Stephen returned to London, he displayed an abundance of gold, silver, jewels, and costly robes," Charles continued. "His coronation is at Westminster Abbey on the day after Christ Mass."

My thoughts went quickly to my children and Adelaide, whose time to deliver our child neared and I would not be present. I prayed they were in no danger.

The messenger looked at me. "Sir Geoffrey, Dowager Queen Adeliza and your heirs have been removed to Arundel where they are in safe hands." Relief flooded my soul for a moment before anger took over.

"Stephen will live to regret this move," I hissed. "Retaliation will be swift and deadly."

"Many ports are closed and guarded in England. I fear you have no recourse, my lord." My shoulders and spirit sank.

The man shuffled his feet and looked at me.

"Do you have more news?"

"Aye, Sir Geoffrey. I was told to report that a Lady Adelaide has delivered a child."

My heart hitched. "Tell me more, kind sir."

"The child is a healthy but delicate lass with a shock of red hair," he added, studying my red hair. I held tight to my emotions with a false face until I was alone and let loose a grin.

17

Matilda delivered our third son in a quiet manner with no fanfare to raise further attention to her vulnerability or that of our youngest son, William. Her forces operated out of the border region where she had established her household knights and estates around Argentan. After a short time of peace, we heard Stephen formed an army to reclaim Argentan Castle with his mercenary forces and local Norman barons loyal to the crown. This news distressed me and I hoped for a detailed report.

Mortecai soon arrived at my camp with welcomed news. "Norman forces deserted King Stephen and he conceded the campaign, Sir Geoffrey."

"By what cause, Cai?"

"When King Stephen attempted to take full control of the anarchy in Normandy he closed in on Lady Matilda's fortress at Argentan and his army—some Flemish mercenaries and others Norman barons—fought amongst themselves and disintegrated before his eyes." Mortecai's own eyes sparkled with the news. "Sir Geoffrey, the king has retreated to England."

"Worthy news, Cai. Thank you for the report." I gave him a nod and a healthy smile. "But I fear for my lady wife and our third son there."

"The new babe is in good hands, my lord. Your squire, Leofrick, slipped in to Argentan and took your infant son, William, with him across the channel, down the coast, and up the River Arun to Arundel to safety with his brothers and the dowager queen."

No doubt surprise showed on my face that Matilda had entrusted the infant with a "mere" squire.

"And the dowager's attendants?"

"They are there, my lord. Even Lady Adelaide has returned to the dowager with an infant."

I could feel my shoulders release an abundance of tension.

"My lord, Lady Matilda's position further improved when her half-brother, Robert of Gloucester—a powerful Anglo-Norman baron— renounced the king and pledged his allegiance to her. Along with his support, she gained a mighty army."

"Splendid news!"

"Not for Gloucester, I fear," Mortecai added with a frown. "Earl Robert's declaration caused a regional rebellion in Kent and across southwest England. I hasten to add that the seeds of civil war have been sown. While Lady Matilda remains in Normandy with Robert on her side, her will to make a move strengthens."

"Civil war? What do you know of this?"

"Your lady wife has attracted a small but powerful coalition of barons in addition to Earl Robert. Their lands lay in borderlands between England and Wales. Their defection from King Stephen has split England in two. To avenge his lack of support, King Stephen himself sped through England with fresh troops, who swore loyalty to his cause, and seized castles and lands belonging to Gloucester." Mortecai stepped closer to me. "And King David of Scotland launched another attack in the north, but his aging forces were no match for King Stephen's swift troops once they arrived."

"Alas, Gloucester and her uncle have supported her cause with fierce loyalty," I said.

Rumors flew that Stephen's army was divided across the continent and the king agreed to a truce with us, he and his forces near exhaustion. I took advantage. He along with Roger of Salisbury organized payment to me of two thousand marks a year in exchange for peace along the Norman border. Even though I had no trust in Stephen, Roger was considered a man of the highest integrity of any in the realm. The offer was worthy. My men and I were battle-weary. Our resources were thin as well. I accepted the offer and the king returned to England and I to Matilda. Peace ruled again but only for a brief period.

Word spread that Matilda was not after peace at all but rather was an invading enemy to England. She now needed her brother most to take her fight into the heart of Stephen's kingdom. Her uniquely royal blood—despite being female— was the sole hope of challenging the sanctity of Stephen's coronation. And Matilda knew Bishop Nigel of Ely and Bishop Roger of Salisbury, King Henry's former chief minister, still controlled the chancery and exchequer. She needed them on her side.

By midyear my lady wife sent a messenger to Rome in hopes Pope Innocent II would throw moral and political support her way. Bishop Ulger of Angers, who represented the pope, told the Second Lateran Council in the Holy City that Stephen had usurped the throne of England, which was Matilda's by right. Over the next fortnight word came that Stephen displayed paranoia and was summoned by his own brother—whom the king had not appointed as archbishop—to appear at council on charges that he had taken improper liberties with the church. Even though nothing came of the Council, it appeared mistrust now surrounded Stephen.

A multitude of messengers were exhausted in an attempt to keep me abreast of each day's challenges while Matilda and I were apart. George of Toulouse stumbled at my feet but offered me yet more news from both Normandy and England. "Your lady wife took advantage of King Stephen's weakened position and traveled by sea to a castle at Arundel, the home of Dowager Queen Adeliza."

"My lady wife is in Castle Arundel?"

"Aye, my lord. Having heard of her daughter-in-law's predicament, the dowager invited Lady Matilda to land at Arundel with Earl Robert and a force of mailed knights, Sir Geoffrey. Lady Matilda headed in darkness for Arundel, overlooking its own port on the navigable river of Arun, five miles from the sea."

"I know of Arundel."

"Leofrick had built a barge for her quiet arrival. The dowager queen is said to have told Lady Matilda that out of respect for her dead husband, who chose her as his heir, she would support her claim and aid in any way she could. Lady Matilda is now under the same roof as the royal children."

"My gratitude for this news goes deep. Go and partake of nourishment and rest before you travel more." George nodded and stumbled towards a bed in the stables. "And take a bath before you leave. Your horse will be rested and groomed as well," I shouted in his direction.

I prayed my lady wife and my mistress in close quarters would not present conflict. I doubted Matilda cared enough to bother Adelaide or the baby, but the events placed the dowager in an awkward circumstance indeed.

<u>18</u>

In late summer a man on pilgrimage came my way to disclose the latest news.

"Sir, Lady Matilda stayed at Arundel while Earl Robert marched northwest with their forces."

"I have been informed of this," I said with little patience.

"But, Sir Geoffrey, King Stephen then moved his troops south, besieged Arundel and trapped Lady Matilda inside the impregnable castle."

"Curses!" My concern for my family nearly took my breath away.

"Ah, my lord, but King Stephen released Lady Matilda and her household knights. His own brother, Bishop Henry, escorted them to reunite with Earl Robert."

I must have stared at the bearer of this news, thunderstruck as I was. I had heard Stephen lived by the Code of Chivalry and mayhap he preferred not to battle a castle of women of high standing, but my suspicions made me even more wary of his actions.

"I am certain my lady wife used the opportunity to her advantage."

"Aye, my lord, she did," the pilgrim responded. "Lady Matilda proceeded to negotiate with the bishop. Around this time many men, ill-tested by Stephen's constant warring, declared themselves *her* supporters, chief among them Brien fitzCount, and Miles of Gloucester."

I knew Matilda considered Brien a chivalrous champion and Miles a military authority. "They will champion her cause. What more can you tell me?"

"Miles surrounded King Stephen's army and killed many of his men and imprisoned many more. A harried King Stephen raced towards London to protect his capital." The pilgrim coughed raggedly.

"Come inside and eat and drink while you tell me more." I motioned the weary man towards the door.

"Thank you, sir. I must admit I haven't eaten." The man's smile grew large at the table spread with many fruits, breads and cheeses. He poured himself a cup of wine and gulped it all, barely allowing it to touch his lips. Wiping his mouth on his sleeve, he continued.

"Lady Matilda moved to the royal fortress at Gloucester owned by her brother to separate herself from the children, for their safety, my lord. I heard King Stephen marched north with an army and met King David, where a compromise was agreed upon. Shortly after, a revolt in southern Wales forced the king to capture Lord Baldwin de Revieres, who was then released to travel to Normandy, where he began a campaign opposing the king's advances."

"Lord Baldwin would be a welcomed force. Much news. It seems the usurping king runs himself in circles."

"Indeed, sir. The king seems weary of battle."

"As am I. What news of the dowager queen and my sons?"

"They are safe at Arundel. King Stephen finds them no threat."

"'Tis music to my ears. What is your name, friend?"

"I am Charles of Tours, at your service."

"Fill your belly and stay the night if you wish."

"Thank you for the hospitality, Sir Geoffrey. I am glad to be the bearer of good tidings."

✤ ✤ ✤

Dafyd, another messenger rode in fast.

"Sir Geoffrey," the man began, knocking hardened mud from his legs and feet as he dismounted near me. "The king of England is imprisoned!"

"Enter and give me details, Dafyd."

He continued as he followed me inside.

"At a final point in the battle at Wallingford, Earl Robert's cavalry linked up with Ranulf of Chester and encircled Stephen, surrounding him with the Angevin army. His personal bravery is well-known but the foolhardy king fought on foot long after much of his army fled. He was concussed and distraught over a multitude of desertions and Earl Robert of Gloucester accosted him with ease, I am told. Lady Matilda met with him at her court in Gloucester and ordered Stephen imprisoned at the fortified castle of Bristol."

I walked away and turned back to Dafyd. "And it has taken far too long to reach a place where my lady wife is within reach of the throne. Let us drink to celebrate!" I roused my men and the other messenger and we feasted and celebrated the king's declining status.

✤ ✤ ✤

The following fortnight I took my troops and began to negotiate peace and annexation of the duchy on my lady wife's behalf while she sought support she needed from the king's brother, Bishop Henry of Winchester.

Mortecai thundered towards me in a field before darkness fell.

"I bring good news, my lord. The clergy—torn between loyalties—welcomed your lady wife into the cathedral where King Stephen had been crowned and named her 'Lady of England'. All that is left to do is proceed to Westminster, take control and rule the country in her own right." Mortecai's gapped horse teeth spread from one ear to the other.

"Matilda stands on the brink of becoming England's first queen!" I yelled out to my men. They became boisterous at the news.

"'Tis only fitting, my lord, with Anglo-Saxon blood from her mother and Norman blood from her grandfather, William the Conqueror," Mortecai leaned in to say with a wink.

My smile broadened and my heart skipped beats. "Let us finish our business here so England and Normandy are all under our control. We will celebrate in earnest when peace comes at last!"

19

Matilda set about to be crowned queen, which required agreement of the Church and her coronation at Westminster Abbey. I hastened to be by her side for support while my men stayed behind to keep our Norman gains untouched. As I journeyed, the lands became more unrecognizable, the curse of years of exhausting battle.

❖ ❖ ❖

When I arrived, my lady wife and I visited the bishop together. Matilda and I bowed. I remained silent as my lady wife made her stand. "Henry of Blois, Bishop of Winchester, you are Stephen's brother, but I implore you as my cousin to deliver support of the Church firmly into my hands."

"For what cause?"

"In exchange for granting you control over all Church affairs," Matilda stated, knowing how ambitious a man he was. He threw up his head and gave her an attentive look. "We have conversed on this matter before."

"I remember," the bishop answered as he rubbed his chin and contemplated her generous offer. "I will take your request under advisement." He then dismissed us with no further conversation.

The council of royal nobles met on the morrow, the majority I heard, against "hateful and arrogant" Matilda's ascension to the English throne. I gulped down bile, hoping she could overcome her own vile disposition. However, the bishop supported her endeavors for his own gains.

During the sinnight she prepared for a coronation unlike any the world had before seen, she became insufferably arrogant and swatted heads, hurting her own cause and alienating almost all who sought to support her. At the moment when the kingdom lay within her grasp, she became intolerable. I pleaded with her to befriend all clergy and citizens of London, but she failed to show respect to chief men throughout the whole kingdom and set about to raise taxes to an unreasonable amount. Her arrogance was now on full display. If questioned, she blazed into unbearable fury, again the despicable woman I knew so well.

Word of this behavior reached Bishop Henry whose hopes were predicated on imposing his own influence on her rule. He demanded Stephen's personal estates be committed to Stephen's twelve-year-old son, Eustace, as long as Stephen remained in prison. Matilda refused, and in so doing, enraged the bishop who at once plotted against her.

I agreed she should not turn over lands to Stephen's young son but Bishop Henry always had ulterior motives of his own. He wanted a degree of control over royal policy far beyond what *any* monarch would tolerate. But her treatment of the English people disturbed me most.

"You have made fools of the citizens, lords and nobles— many sainted people who welcomed you back to London. You have shown no respect or gratitude to clergy for their much-needed support. You have, through your ever-present arrogance and entitlement, turned them away, never I fear to pledge their allegiance to you again!"

My lady wife's brow furrowed. "Hold your tongue with me, Geoffrey!" She stared at me with viciousness and crossed her arms over her chest as though they were impenetrable armor.

Our usual impasse followed.

❖ ❖ ❖

King David arrived without an army, and as he entered, Matilda refused to stand and recognize the king, her uncle. His face reddened and his fists bulged as he approached her. He begged his niece to be a gentle and kind-hearted leader.

"England is now Norman, Lady Matilda, and not bound by its Anglo-Saxon past. Monarchs are expected to be soldiers, warriors! While your royal blood gives you right to the throne, your sex impedes you. You must see that," King David was bold enough to say to his niece. "The empire is most unstable. Your countenance is highly noted and there seems little respect for you."

"Respect? My father required his nobles to swear a solemn oath that they would uphold my right and that of any sons I birthed. They swore it in *public*," she hissed. "There is the respect!"

"You are foolhardy, Matilda, if you think that is all it takes to be respected!" The king's voice grew louder.

My lady wife now stood and walked over to her uncle and had the audacity to box his ear with the ill temper of a cornered badger. "I am *quite* aware of my sex, Uncle," she huffed, glaring at me as if she hoped I would dare interfere in her tirade.

King David grabbed his ear in noticeable pain with a look of shock on his face. Her rabid demeanor shocked even me.

The King of Scotland pulled his dagger and approached her face, getting nose to nose with her. "I have no more

words for you, menacing Matilda! I have done nought but
support your cause, and you box my ear? I have put my life
and my train in danger oft times for you and you act in this
manner?" His face turned crimson. "In all your haughtiness,
you refuse to stand and recognize a king? If you were a
man, I would disembowel you here and now!" The king
hissed at her and stomped past me before turning back to
her. "You, my ungrateful and condescending niece, regard
yourself too highly and without merit. Your effrontery I
will tolerate no longer. I return to Scotland and you will see
me no more." The enraged king stomped from the room
and slammed the huge door behind him.

"Matilda!" My vexed voice echoed in the chamber.

She threw her palm in my direction and dared me to
scold her. Nought I could say would persuade her to
compassion, but I had to attempt reconciliation between
them.

"Go after your uncle and make amends, I beg you. You
can ill afford to have him your enemy. You need his troops."

Nor would she hear of freeing Stephen, although he
had vowed to leave and never attempt to be king again.

"I beseech you, Matilda, free the man. And go after
your uncle and make amends. If you dare not, I fear—"

"You fear much, Geoffrey! What has become of your
courage?"

"What has become of your *sanity*? Your wits are in
abeyance!" I barked back. "Even the English are now in
favor with Stephen and call you an evil shrew. ''Twill not
end well."

"Leave if you have not the courage to stand with me.
The inheritance which is mine by right I will then obtain by
force. I need you not!" She spit out the words.

I could not have removed myself from Matilda's
presence with more swiftness. I said nothing but packed
and left, glad my sons were with Adelaide and Queen Adeliza

out of this madness. I was pleased the dowager queen had become quite attached to the lads and to Adelaide.

With those I loved out of harm's way, I nevertheless sent Dafyd to assess the situation and report back to me in Normandy. Each time he returned with more intriguing stories about my lady wife and her pursuits.

One evening a breathless Dafyd dismounted and began his latest saga about my lady wife. "Despite Lady Matilda's lingering support, mercenary forces loyal to Stephen—ordered by his lady wife Matilde—remained close to the city. Matilde begged her brother-in-law, Bishop Henry, not to recognize Lady Matilda's claim but instead to release her husband from prison. William of Ypres marched from Kent to the Thames, mere miles from Lady Matilda and the Palace of Westminster. Stephen's army, under orders from Matilde herself, waged war on London with plunder, arson, and violence, Sir Geoffrey."

"Most foul news, Dafyd."

"With goading from Stephen's loyalists and while your lady wife dined, bells tolled and the gates opened. London rose up against Lady Matilda and swarmed in with weapons in hand and forced her to horse and retreat to Oxford."

"Where is she now?"

"Gloucester, my lord. But there is more news. Robert of Gloucester was captured by Stephen's army and imprisoned."

"All is lost without Earl Robert," I said.

"There is more still, my lord," Dafyd said, reaching his hand out towards my arm. "Plans were made to exchange King Stephen for Earl Robert. Stephen is now a free man again."

My heart sank. I caught my head in my hands. My groan was audible to all in the hall. Mayhap Matilda's chance to become queen had disappeared forever and taken our son's chance of the throne along with it.

20

After more skirmishes in Normandy and in much need of a respite, I slipped across the channel to Arundel and waited for Adelaide to enter the bedchamber. I sprawled naked on the bed, my broad shoulders at one end and my long legs off the other end. When she entered she would in an instant know how much I wanted her, needed her.

I heard the door swish open and watched as a lovely vision peeked around.

"Geoffrey Plantagenet! You are elegantly arrogant!" She laughed and rushed to me, dropping her chemise as she ran.

"Unloose your locks, my love." The beautiful creature I loved dearly stopped, naked just out of my reach, and pulled the pins from her hair, letting it cascade over her breasts as her face flushed.

"Does this embarrass you?"

"I prefer darkness for my nakedness, Geoffrey."

"And I prefer light to take in all of your beauty."

She stepped closer and I pulled her to me, wrapping her in my arms. We both giggled like small children who had a secret to keep. My hardness left no question of my neediness.

Our bodies tangled and twisted in love and lust, both of us touching each other over and over again in ways that made me want to scream out. And then we trembled into a long combined climax and lay back, spent and enchanted.

Breathlessly, Adelaide turned to me. "You are dangerous, my lord."

"Do you fear me?"

"Only if fear means that I want to spend all daylights and night times in your arms," she whispered. She pushed up to kiss my lips. "You are a noble man, Geoffrey. You are kind, loving, and of high integrity. You are passionate and tender, even though you are sometimes impatient and do not take 'no' for an answer."

"You would deny me?"

She laughed and patted my leg. I smiled down at her, flopped back on the bed and fell fast asleep. When I woke, Adelaide was gone. While I could stay in bed, she had duties with the dowager queen and my sons. I felt guilt slide across my head, and clamored off the bed and into my clothes, hungry now for a different kind of nourishment. I had lost weight over the course of long battles and felt stronger now in the arms of my beloved and away from the constant melee in which Matilda found herself.

In the early morn, I crept stealthily down the corridor until I saw a crouching darkness ahead. A low growl grew stronger and the huge creature bared its fangs as I stopped and reached for my dagger, only to remember I had left it beside my bed. The beast let out a terrifying noise and I cowered with no protection but my arms and legs.

"I see you've met Goliath," I heard Adelaide call out behind me. I didn't turn towards her voice but kept my eyes on the beast slowly moving closer to me.

Adelaide came up beside me. "Silence, Goliath. This man will not hurt us. He protects us as you do," she said softly. The growling ceased and by now light aided my vision enough to see the mastiff that could have been my undoing.

I glanced at Adelaide.

"Leofrick got him for extra protection."

"You could have warned me."

"I had no thought of him. I felt protected in your arms, Geoffrey. Please forgive me."

How could I not?

21

In the fall season, I invaded a war-weary Normandy again
and conquered the entire duchy south of the River Seine
and east of the Risle with little effort. Stephen might be
back in power in England, but Normandy would not be
his! Just as I had hoped, my success in Normandy and
Stephen's weakness in England influenced the loyalty of
any Anglo-Norman barons who feared losing lands in
England to Matilda and possessions in Normandy to me.
Castle after castle surrendered.

But the fickle Henry of Blois transferred his support
back to his brother and reaffirmed Stephen's legitimacy to
rule. A fresh coronation occurred. Robert of Gloucester
refused to change his loyalty to Stephen and returned to
Matilda.

By winter of that year Robert came to Normandy to
assist me with operations against some of Stephen's
remaining followers. But after he arrived we heard Matilda
had come under pressure from Stephen's forces and was
surrounded at Oxford when he led a sudden attack across
the river, stormed the town, and trapped her in the castle.
Robert attempted to hasten back to England but foul
weather kept him from crossing the channel with young
Henry.

Mortecai rode into camp one day to report my lady wife's latest predicament.

"Since the castle is well-fortified, Stephen decided to settle down for a long siege and starve out your lady wife. He hindered food and supplies from being brought to Lady Matilda. In a raw winter like this, 'tis certain all necessities were depleted in haste."

"Matilda needs my assistance?"

"No, my lord," he continued. "One night a blizzard covered the ground and filled the darkness with flakes. 'Tis told she and three of her knights dressed in white and lowered themselves down the castle wall with ropes. No one saw them in blinding snow as they walked across the frozen Thames and escaped to fitzCount's castle at Wallingford."

I could not conceal the smile forming on my face. "Matilda is a devious one!"

❖ ❖ ❖

By winter's end, my lady wife had rebuilt her court at Devizes Castle in Wiltshire—one of the stateliest in Europe—and established her knights on surrounding estates supported by mercenaries and ruled through a network of local sheriffs. Those who had lost lands held by King Stephen traveled to take up patronage from Matilda.

"Nevertheless, the last news I heard, my lord, is that negotiations with clergy and nobility rendered Stephen with the kingdom. Stephen remains undisputed King of England, Sir Geoffrey. A stalemate has been reached; neither the king nor Lady Matilda has a strong enough army left to destroy the other."

22

Within a fortnight the Earl of Essex rebelled against Stephen in East Anglia and based himself on the Isle of Ely, where he began a military campaign against Cambridge and planned to progress south towards London. That was all the impetus I needed to complete my mission.

With little use of force, I secured my hold on Normandy Seine and advanced to Rouen where King Louis VIII of France recognized me as Duke of Normandy. Even with my own military success, Matilda could not consolidate her position. Stephen attacked and killed the Earl of Essex at Burwell Castle, moved against Matilda's weakened forces and managed to recapture Oxfordshire.

A messenger thundered up to me as I trotted across a hillock.

"Your lady wife has lost her chance to rule England, Sir Geoffrey, but she makes plans to see her son, Henry, recognized as the male heir who embodies all hereditary rights to the throne. She now plans to focus on teaching him how to rule as her father did."

I nodded in silence.

Over the course of the next year, several of Matilda's key supporters died. Miles of Gloucester was killed by a stray arrow while hunting. Earl Robert died of a fever. Later Brien fitzCount died, but I was never told in what manner.

Others joined the Second Crusade, many wanting no further conflict. After mourning these great supporters, Matilda returned to Normandy, where she settled into a quieter life, her resolve to be queen at last depleted. She knew the aging king's power was crumbling but she could do little to take advantage.

At a later date I would cede the duchy to young Henry, but, for a time, I wanted to enjoy the rewards earned from years of battle scars, both physical and emotional. Leofrick went to Arundel Castle and brought the dowager queen, Adelaide, our daughter, Emme, and my three sons to me at Loches Castle. Their arrival was a joyous occasion, indeed.

❖ ❖ ❖

Summers came and went as I ruled as Duke of Normandy. I attended to peaceful duties and observed my royal sons grow and play with Adelaide's Emme whose countenance I could not deny and never would. Even with Matilda's cousin as King of England, I worked tirelessly in the negotiation of all issues between Normandy and England to insure our son Henry would succeed him.

On a beautiful hot day fitzHildebrand, a messenger from the Far East, arrived with a dispatch from my father, Fulk V, King of Jerusalem, requesting my assistance to capture Demascus and secure the northern border. I called my men together and told Blou and Hardouin to prepare for our long journey. I then summoned Leofrick.

"M' lord?"

"Frick, I will be away with my men in Jerusalem. I leave you here to guard and protect Queen Adeliza, the royal heirs, and Lady Adelaide."

He dropped his head, disappointment on his face.

"Come closer," I gestured to him.

"Aye, m'lord," he said, stepping forward.

"Because you are a strong, honorable and loyal man, I hereby name you Leofrick, Count of Anjou."

My squire's head shot up. "M'lord! I am honored. I have never been from any place." His eyes teared. "At last I belong! I will protect all here at all cost, sir."

"I know you will. I would trust you with my *own* life, Frick. Protect those I love. I will return, but it may be a long absence. I know you would do honorable battle with me, but my most precious treasures I leave under your care."

"Aye, m'lord."

I said my farewells to my Norman family, kissed my sons and beautiful Emme, and gave Adelaide a lingering kiss. I wiped tears from her eyes.

"Fret not. I will return."

"Godspeed, Geoffrey," she whispered before I mounted up with my men.

❖ ❖ ❖

We were fortunate to have summer's sun for most of the lengthy journey and camped under stars most nights, with rain in short supply until we neared Antioch.

There heavy rain set upon us and kept us in our tents with no promise of travel. From my tent flap I peered out at unrelenting rain and puddles, pools and even fast water seemed determined to flood our camp and hold us hostage on the side of a mountain.

"My Lord Geoffrey," yelled Hardouin, dashing past me into the tent, "I fear the mountain behind us gives way. We must leave this place."

"Har—"

"Now, my lord!"

I knew his tone well enough to grab my gear and run to our picket of horses. We mounted up and abandoned camp. As we galloped away, we heard a mighty roar and looked over our shoulders as sodden earth raced downhill to bury our camp. We bolted to rock and made our way to the top, having survived being buried alive with only our mounts and a handful of supplies left. We stayed along the ridge until rain became a mist and earth became solid enough to carry the weight of our mounts again.

My father sent a guide to show us the safest way to the Crusader state of Damascus, where we joined forces with his small army, just dealt a defeat in battle near Baarin.

After planning a military strategy with Hardouin and the king, we captured the fort of Banias to the north of Lake Tiberias, thus securing the northern border with ease.

"My son," Fulk said as we celebrated victory, "I need for you to stay and help strengthen the southern border."

I said nought.

He continued. "Much has transpired since you left. As you are aware, even though the throne of Jerusalem was rightfully Melisende's, I as an experienced military commander, assumed sole control of the government . . . with her consent."

I dipped my head and smiled.

He sighed deeply. "However, much conflict with other rulers and a brief battle with Hugues II of Le Priset changed my position on the matter. 'Tis very unpleasant, indeed, since Hugues and I were once allies. To return to peace, I forfeited direct control over government matters back to Melisende." His ruddy complexion reddened.

"I am sorry, Father."

"I am quite content, but I implore you to help strengthen Jerusalem's borders. We are a small and weak force. I am in dire need of your assistance to secure the southern borders. A fortress will be erected at Kerak, east of the Dead Sea, giving the kingdom access to the Red Sea."

He took my shoulders in his hands and looked me in the eye.

"You will join the Knights Templar, my son, if Hugues of Payen gives his approval."

"It would be a high honor, Father."

"Hugues created this elite force of nine men to protect pilgrims on their way to the Holy Land. Now more sons of nobility will be recruited, you among them."

My father alongside my stepmother, Queen Melisende, subsidized the Knights Templar. He maintained two knights in the Holy Land to protect pilgrims from robbers on The Crusades, while seven others roamed the realm. To become a Knight Templar was a high honor, but even with such honor, I knew where my heart and responsibilities lay.

"I dare not be away from Normandy at length, Father."

"Normandy and England are at peace now, my son. This kingdom is not yet secure. " My father's dark eyes seemed to pierce my head and heart.

"Mayhap we can aid you, but only for a while."

My father smiled and patted both of my shoulders.

"I know I can count on you, my son. And Normandy counts on you. And there are royal heirs who count on you. You are a capable warrior who has earned great respect. Hardouin and Blou are esteemed as well."

"Yet neither has been knighted," I added.

His head lifted. "Mayhap knighthood soon awaits them."

✤ ✤ ✤

My men and I stayed and helped build the fortress at Kerak and began the erections of several new forts in the southwest part of the kingdom to overpower the Egyptian fortress at Ascalon.

Once Fulk felt more secure, he knighted Hardouin and

Blou and we made the long journey back to Normandy where the sentry announced our arrival.

"Sir Geoffrey Plantagenet, Duke of Normandy, Sir Hardouin of Saint-Mars and Sir Robert of Blou."

"Knights all, m'lord?" Frick asked as we dismounted.

"Knights all, Count LeoFrick." I looked him over. "You became a man while I was abroad."

He grinned. "All is well here, m'lord. Others grew, as you shall see."

I threw out my arms as Henry ran to me, young Geoffrey and William close behind him. I picked them up and swung them around nearly stumbling under their weight.

"You are no longer babes and a load for my arms," I said to them. "Take the horses to the stables, lad, and we can unpack after the gloaming," I directed Henry, who had grown to reach my own eyes.

"I will go with them, m'lord, and *we* shall unpack," Frick said, gesturing behind him where Adelaide stood, holding a long-legged, curly-haired angel. I ran to them, kissing Adelaide with great passion before looking at our daughter.

"Emme is an armful as well." I took her but she whimpered and scrambled to get down and run to a nursemaid.

"Forgive her, Geoffrey. She knows you not," Adelaide spoke in a soft voice.

I kissed her lips and clung to her.

"I have missed you so, my fair Adelaide, but I stink," I confessed.

"The nursemaid will tend the children while I join you in the River Maine."

"Splendid!"

✣ ✣ ✣

As we approached the river bank, I gawked at hewn timber turning in the water east of us.

"'Tis another project of Count Leofrick," Adelaide explained.

"A mill?"

"Water powers it. Our grains are now milled here, corn, wheat, and barley for the castle."

"The lad from muck proves himself more useful by the day," I said before disrobing and diving into the water.

We swam and splashed about playfully in the cool river before we bathed each other. Our absence from one another was answered long before darkness drove us into the bedchamber.

"The bed is inviting, indeed," I said.

"Fleas invaded the straw so Count Leofrick ordered fresh rushes for all beds, layered thick, and my dear Queen Adeliza covered them in soft linen."

"My weary bones will sleep well," I said, reaching for my lady, "but later." Our limbs intertwined and unbridled passion flowed freely. Our childhood friendship had endured long privations and seasons of separation, but our love stayed the course. I had never felt so blessed.

Later I collapsed on the new bed. "I am bone weary."

"Rest well, my precious knight." She kissed me once again with great tenderness.

✦ ✦ ✦

On the morrow I visited the dowager queen.

"You are well?"

"I am well and content, Sir Geoffrey. The children are a joy to me, and I must confess Lady Adelaide behaves nobly in your absence. 'Tis a pleasure to have such company."

"I expected nothing less," I said.

"She adores you and you her. You deserved more than you had with Matilda. I am happy for you."

I smiled. "Have you heard from her?"

"I send messages to *her*, indicating how the heirs fare. She seems only concerned with Henry, but I report on the others as well. She keeps to herself at the priory at Notre Dame, I have heard. Mayhap she finds her own peace there."

"I trust she does. I am pleased, Queen Adeliza, although I fear robust negotiation will be necessary for Henry to ascend the throne which rightly he should." I rose to go. "Has peace remained in Normandy during my absence?"

"Indeed. Count Leofrick would take on an army alone and win," she said with a soft laugh. "How I do adore him. We have talked at length. It seems he has no father or mother and knows not from whence he came. His life before the Palace at Westminster was of fear, abuse, and loneliness. You have done a fine deed to take him in, Geoffrey."

"Frick has done far more for me. His talents amaze me. Paieri found him and we have all been obliged. He does no less here in Normandy."

23

Castle attendants and squires decorated my Loches Hall at Christ Mass with festive decorations to celebrate Saint Nicholas. Pine and fir boughs provided scents I loved for the season. Jacquelin had left King Stephen and come to Normandy, and other cooks picked the best fresh meats from town butchers and selected fruits, nuts and flours that would bake into sweet and aromatic breads and pastries. Aromas from the kitchen made my mouth water.

"Sir Geoffrey, what a banquet we shall have," Jacquelin announced as he turned a spit in the kitchen fireplace, crane the meat of choice. "I brought new spices from the palace grounds in England. Some are mild and others robust."

I smiled at his excitement. "I look forward to the feast you prepare and to sharing it all with Lady Adelaide, the dowager queen, my children and all of you." I knew he was most contented when he prepared banquets of complexity and reveled in compliments thereafter.

Jacquelin pulled me from my thoughts. "I have a sugary surprise in store for the dowager queen." He told me of his plan and I agreed that mayhap his creation might make her first feast in Normandy a festive occasion.

And much celebration there would be. The castle was a flurry of activity as final preparations were made. The children helped their grandmother decorate a huge tree in the hall and Adelaide was directing the placement of greenery throughout the castle when I walked up behind her. When she turned, she bowed discreetly and I remained still only through strong will. Our eyes danced but we only smiled and said nothing. Later we all broke fast and feasted on quail eggs, ham and sweet bread.

"I do not wish to eat much," Adelaide said in my direction. "I want to savor the main feast at noontide." I smiled, looking past her at the dowager queen, who ate even less and did not engage in conversation. I later walked the women back to their chambers, holding on to the dowager's arm and gently rubbing my mistress's arm.

"Are you well, Queen Adeliza?"

"Even though time passes, my heart still grieves, Sir Geoffrey. The Feast of Saint Nicholas is a difficult time for me since my beloved husband died in this season."

I nodded. "How can I, in some manner, soften your grief?"

She forced a smile and reached for my hand. "You are a worthy man, Sir Geoffrey, with many charges on your shoulders. I will mend as seasons come and go. You take excellent care of me and my needs. I am forever grateful."

"'Tis my great pleasure to see you are well-tended, Queen Adeliza. Rest, but you must come to the main feast at noontide. I trust you will find it uplifting," I told her.

"Then I shall rest and join you." Her smile was genuine. Her eyes, even though cloudy, held much gratitude. I turned slightly, blocking Adelaide's steps.

"When can I see you? Our child?"

"At the feast, Sir Geoffrey," she said and ducked under my arm and out of sight.

Later an elder knight escorted Dowager Queen Adeliza in her royal finery to the Hall and Lady Adelaide and I followed, bedecked in our festive best, my children close behind us with attendants for the younger ones. The hall filled with knights, barons, dukes, earls, squires and attendants. I did not catch sight of Leofrick in their midst.

Beautifully-displayed foods were set before us. And we each threw a long cloth over our left shoulders to wipe greasy hands. We ate with great pleasure; even the dowager queen seemed to have found her appetite.

"Oh!" Henry let out a delighted response to finding the bean cooked inside his bread. "I am King of the Bean!"

"You will be crowned king of the holiday feast, my son," the dowager announced, nodding to a servant who brought forth an unadorned golden crown to set upon my son's head.

"This is the first of many crowns you will wear," I called out to him.

Our pewter plates were removed and music began to play. We all turned to see Jacquelin place a board in front of the dowager queen. The board held a magnificent tiered white cake adorned with golden spun sugar.

Although I could not read the face of the king's widow, we enjoyed cake and broke off pieces of sugar—some for Henry and the other children—before our attendants consumed the rest. I watched Adelaide lick each of her fingertips as though they alone were the highlight of the feast. I longed to lick the fingers for her but instead turned my attention back to the children. We then exchanged gifts. I had ordered a great tapestry made for Lady Adelaide's private chamber wall, woven in exquisite colors by the newly-established guild nearby.

"Geoffrey, I will treasure this glorious art and it will enliven my chamber. Thank you."

"I am pleased you are pleased, my lady."

Dowager Queen Adeliza received gifts that filled the table before her and she smiled with modesty and nodded her gratitude to each giver. I gave Frick a nod and he and another man brought in a heavy gift and set it down in front of the dowager. She jumped up with delight.

"A treadle loom! Oh, how I have longed for one."

"To create your own woven designs," I announced with pride. "I am happy that you are pleased." She beamed at me and walked around the table to inspect the device.

The celebration of Saint Nicholas ended and the Hall cleared. I touched Adelaide's arm and handed her another gift, wrapped in sumptuous silk. "For you," I whispered.

She removed the silk and ran her fingertips across metallic embossing. "'Tis a leather book?" She opened it to blank pages and gave me a quizzical look. "There is nought written within its pages, Geoffrey."

"'Tis for you to write your *own* story," I explained.

"I will fill its pages with sentiments of you and our child, Geoffrey. 'Tis a treasure. Thank you."

"And I have enlisted an antiquary to teach you calligraphy," I whispered.

She beamed. "Oh, I have long wished to write with flair."

I laughed and helped her up from the table, looking forward to a feast of another nature after darkness.

24

Henry, now fourteen summers, had grown into a handsome lad with golden red hair, a freckled face, his grandfather's stockiness and his great grandfather's magnetic personality. When I was fortunate enough to be near him, sometimes I caught myself staring with envy and pride. Under Matilda's tutelage he would assume a leading role in the workings of Norman government, and if the need arose, enter conflicts on the home front.

After a brief journey to Rouen, I summoned my oldest son to the stables. When he did not come, I called out to Frick, "I have sent for Henry and he has not appeared."

"M'lord," Leofrick said, kicking dirt with his boot, "he is gone and without permission."

"Gone?"

"I fear to England, m'lord, after assembling a band of rogues."

"Across the channel to England? For what purpose?"

"To take that which he feels entitled to, m'lord."

I threw down my gear and walked towards Frick. "The *throne*?"

Frick nodded.

"Has he gone mad?" My voice boomed with shock and anger, causing even the horses to flinch. "Why did you allow this?"

"M' lord, he left under the cloak of darkness without my knowledge or permission. He made all his plans in secrecy. I wanted to chase after him, but the family here would be left with no protector in your absence," Frick explained. "Henry has been gone a sinnight."

I sighed and tried to calm down. "'Tis not your fault, Frick. I fear that boy has his mother's stubborn head." I looked at the ground, praying my son would not be injured on his bold adventure. "Who are these rogues you speak of?"

"A small army of lads he rounded up, most near his own years and with no more experience than he owns."

Within hours George of Tours arrived out of breath with news of Henry's exploits.

"Sir Geoffrey, when your son arrived in London, he lacked funds to pay his men. When they began to desert him, he sent a messenger to his mother for funds." He took in a long breath. "Lady Matilda refused her own son, stating years of conflict had left her funds depleted. When the message of refusal arrived back in England, your young Henry, with great bravery . . . or foolishness, appealed to the king himself to pay the troops with agreement that he and his men would return to Normandy."

"What effrontery! My son knows no fear."

"Then, Sir Geoffrey, to the surprise of all, King Stephen himself paid off Henry's men and allowed him to return to Anjou unhindered. He is a short distance behind me." He cocked his head over his shoulder.

"Your news is heard, George. Go and rest. I will be prepared for my son when he dismounts," I said with a cold calm voice that hid my true feelings.

I awaited my son with little patience. Upon his return, as he dismounted, I snatched him roughly by the arms and spun him around to face me. Henry bobbed his head about as I barked at his impulsive act. "King Stephen should have imprisoned you and all your men. You are indeed fortunate to still own your head!" I lifted my hand to strike him but stopped its movement midair and looked into his remorseful eyes.

"Father, you would strike me?" he said as he dropped to one knee and awaited my wrath. "I deserve it."

I looked over the wide-eyed lads who rode in with him. "Disperse to your own homes and lands at once!" My voice bellowed forth and they turned on their mounts and hurried away at full pelt. I reached down and pulled Henry up to stand eye to eye with me.

I motioned him inside. "You are hungry, my son. Let us find nourishment while you explain your imprudent actions."

I listened to my son's innocent and feeble attempts to explain himself and tried to hold my anger at bay. I had once been young and foolish but never had the pluck needed to overthrow a king. I found his behavior somewhat amusing but did not say so.

In the days following, I involved Henry in the monitoring of family lands to keep him occupied on the home front and prepare him for his future, with the hope that, with age, he would understand the ramifications of war, and when no other means presented itself. And, mayhap King Stephen realized young Henry was determined to fight for his inheritance and was, indeed, an impressive lad—scholarly but calm in crisis, although he had much to learn about forming an army and taking to war.

Sadly, what had once been a peaceful England continued to suffer the consequences of years of merciless struggle between Stephen and Matilda. The central government began to disintegrate and greedy barons took property from towns and shires all over England.

Matilda met our three sons and me in Rouen. The years of war had not been kind to her. Together with Henry, Geoffrey, and William, we made arrangements for her future life in Normandy.

"I shall not wear the crown, but our Henry will! My life is now aimed at putting our son on the throne of England. 'Tis all I care about." She transmitted her claim to Henry but continued to actively influence his councils as royal deputy.

Matilda continued to live in the priory where she would focus on the administration of Normandy rather than on war with England. I sent the Bishop of Therouanne to Rome to campaign for Henry's right to the throne of England and the English Church shifted loyalty to him. Over the next months, we made peace with Louis VIII, who then supported Henry's rights to the duchy of Normandy whenever I wished to pass the title to him.

We settled into peace on all fronts.

25

More knights were being recruited from orders of The Angelic Knights, The Thistle of Bourbon, The Wing of Saint Michael, and Knights of the Bath to the Holy Land and protect pilgrims from robbers and murderers and to protect the Temple Mount, with our lives if required. Hardouin, Blou and I traveled alone until we joined a throng of warriors who hoped to meet the requirements of The Knights Templar, one of the greatest military orders of the age, called "Soldiers of Christ" by Christians.

Our long journey was peaceful through Christian lands until Constantinople, where Asia Minor hostilities began. The Turks—led by the evil Zengi—now recognized Christianity as a serious threat and would make attempts to massacre all of our troops.

We followed a train of one-hump camels for a time but we were impatient, and I was ill-spirited at having a cantankerous camel right ahead of me. My mount disliked our position in the train more than I did. He had to go around piles of camel relief. Several times the ornery beast took off with his rider yelling curses and trying to beat him into submission. I soon tugged Honor over and my men and I galloped away from the camel train and caught up with another throng of men mounted on swift horses and tackling the red dunes ahead.

Once we approached a few gnarly trees, we could see throngs of vultures circling something swaying beneath them. Riding closer, we all realized insect-covered bodies of men dangled there, hanged by the neck, some with entrails protruding, mayhap torn open by the large birds. I hastened to turn my head and rode faster and farther away, now scouring the land for the Turks who had left them there. My men swiftly caught up with me. After we survived the Turks, our next foes were drought and famine and the rugged mountains that had taken a toll on many who had travelled before us. When rain came in torrents, it brought treacherous floods through the drought-ravaged mountains and made fording a dangerous, if not impossible, quest.

As we rode, I contemplated becoming a true Templar. Each knight must adopt Benedictine monastic rules and wear white tunics and red crosses. The order emphasized piety, faith, humility, and chastity. I knew not if I could pass the test since I was wed to Matilda even though I had no plans to ever touch her body again. But Adelaide, sweet, passionate Adelaide.

Could I keep a vow to never know *her* again?

One day Heaven's floodgate opened and brought with it bitter gusts of cold wind, hitting us and our mounts head-on. When we turned westward, the gale moved to our backs, pushing us along towards Jerusalem. The storm ended as quickly as it had begun but our clothing was soaked and heavy.

We found my father, Fulk V, and knelt when we reached him. I knew he funded the recruitment enterprise along with the Templar founder and Grand Master Hugues of Payen, overseer of both military forces in the Holy Land and eastern Europe and the Templars' business interests in western Europe.

"Sir Geoffrey Plantagenet," my father whispered, "you and your men need not endure a test. You are well-known as respected warriors from Scotland to Jerusalem. You earn the Templar robes once you adopt Benedictine monastic rules and pledge your allegiance. You, Sir Hardouin of Saint-Mars, and Sir Robert of Blou, will join the military arm of the order of The Temple of Jerusalem and become Knights Templar along with Sir Geoffrey Plantagenet."

"We are honored, Your Grace," we said in unison as we knelt.

We settled in to a small space provided for us to wait for the ceremony. I dozed off and awoke after being shaken about the shoulders.

"Sir Geoffrey Plantagenet?"

I looked into a stranger's eyes.

"I am."

"Come with me. You are summoned by Hugues of Payen."

I looked about me. "All of us?"

"You alone are to follow me."

I followed the man to a huge wooden door and he nodded for me to enter. I knocked and opened the door.

"Sir Plantagenet, you do not meet the criteria to be a Templar," he declared to me in private from across the room. I held my tongue to await the reason for his statement. "Alas, you are wed to Empress Matilda. All know of this. I, Hugues of Payen, attended the marriage."

"I remember, Grand Master." I sighed and stepped towards him. "My lord, my lady wife and I are estranged. We do not live as man and wife."

"It matters not!"

I remained silent as he studied me at close range.

"You are one of the best warrior knights in all the land, Sir Geoffrey. Your ability to use both hands allows you great advantage over most men, large and brutish or small and quick. We need you with us."

"What mean you, my lord?"

"You are fortunate that Bernard, the most noted church father of this time, declared *this* day that the region needed mailed knights ready for active military battle, not a group of wailing monks. You will now be admitted to the military order with my blessing. You are, after all, Fulk's son, but I expect you to remain chaste."

"I assure you I am chaste as far as Matilda is concerned," I announced.

"Then I will not stand in your way," Hugues promised.

I bowed and left, elated at the news, but thoughts of Adelaide crept into my mind. Would she understand?

Hardouin, Blou and I vowed to defend Jerusalem—a beleaguered Holy Land—and were given a house near Solomon's Temple. We donned white surcoats with red crosses and pledged not only to protect the Temple Mount and pilgrims but also to help establish Christian communities throughout the continent. A feast of *boeuf bourguignon* and *coq au vin* served with wine made us lethargic, and we bedded down early.

✤ ✤ ✤

We, along with other well-trained professional soldiers, would become a force to be reckoned with. Over the next year we grew in strength, wealth, influence and prestige. We practiced our skills alone and in groups, an impressive show wherever we went in full harness on stout horses. We seldom had to fight; Intimidation opened most gates and doors. The Knights Templar code of honor was not to be underestimated, but as time passed, we all took part in capturing opposing knights to gain ransom and booty, such as a wealth of armor and magnificent war horses. In all this time I never encountered Zengi, much to my disappointment.

✤ ✤ ✤

When we at last traveled home to Normandy, I took with me concepts from the Holy Land, new ideas in philosophy, military tactics, and medicine. I brought gifts for Queen Adeliza and Lady Adelaide—two rolls of wool carpet to cover the cold stone floors of their private chambers—an array of delicate fabrics, perfume, and toys for the royal heirs and Emme.

I sat beside Adelaide on a blanket and watched the children and dogs at play. The mastiff that had been purchased to guard the children had grown into a huge beast but he played like a pup unless I got close to them. He then growled and snarled at me until Henry patted his head and threw his arm over mine to indicate I was no threat. Henry had grown taller and made decisions for all of his siblings, it seemed, and recognized himself as protector in my absence.

"Henry is made of stern stuff. He will be a great king," I said to the lovely woman beside me.

"He will. He is well-read, good at game tactics and manipulation, and Count Leofrick has taught him archery. They have brought home hart and hare from hunts."

"Count Leofrick can teach him much if he will listen and heed his words." I shifted my gaze to Adelaide. "I should visit Matilda and attend to his future," I added and nodded in my son's direction.

"Must you journey again so soon?" She turned to me. "I have missed you so, Geoffrey, and I am proud that you are a Templar Knight and a respected warrior, although I despise being apart from you. I feel safest in your arms."

I pulled her close to me. "As a Templar I have done little combat, and when we show force, 'tis a short campaign,

Adelaide. Much of our travels have been nothing more than to gather intelligence and tactics. We ride on the reputation of those nine mighty warriors who went before us."

"You are spies?"

"In some regard, but, uppermost, for our own well-being. We advance shock troops in battle to protect pilgrims. We are heavily armored knights on stout war horses who break through enemy lines even before the main army arrives."

"A most dangerous position, Geoffrey."

"I am well-protected and—"

"A worthy warrior," she interrupted.

I smiled. "I become one with my war horses and my trusted men. 'Tis a powerful sensation."

"Do you feel invincible?"

I laughed aloud. "I am safe enough, my dear Adelaide."

"And bronzed by the desert sun. Be brave and strong, Geoffrey, but exhibit no foolishness. You are *still* mortal."

"Can I not act foolish when we are together?" I reached for her.

She pushed me back with both hands, intent on finishing the conversation.

"I have heard the Templars use intimidation and fear tactics to get what they desire, Geoffrey. I have heard these knights have grown arrogant and above laws. They rape, pillage and—"

I put my hands around her face. "Adelaide, some apples rot even in a sack of good ones. Templars are respected in the realm, and those who have forgotten the oath and ravaged and plundered I pray will be weeded out. Our very appearance on stout steeds and in full metal intimidates, and has kept us from maiming many who concede with no force necessary."

She smiled up at me and I put my arm around her and pulled her close to kiss her sweet mouth before speaking again. "I fear my father makes enemies in Jerusalem. He no longer allows towns to administer themselves and vassals in the realm are ill-treated."

"Was that not what caused the upheavals here with barons and vassals who felt you and King Henry did not support them?"

"The same. I fear this will not end well."

I spent time with my former squire and thanked him for caring well for my family in my absence.

"I can in no way repay all you have done for me, Frick."

"M'lord," Frick tilted his head, "you saved a rag from the dung heap and made it a squire and now Count of Anjou. You entrusted me with your most-prized lady and children. You owe me nought. I have conversed with Lady Adelaide on many occasions, and she has allowed me to teach the royal heirs to hunt and to build from wood. She adores you, m'lord."

"And I her, Frick." Adelaide was my mistress not my lady wife, but she had been more family to me than Matilda had ever been.

Frick moved to my side and tapped my elbow with his own. "Now, that Henry of yours is most apt at hunting. Young Geoffrey is best at running circles around us both, and William seems not at all interested in outdoor endeavors."

I laughed heartily. "Geoffrey is young yet. He does seem full of energy and mischief. William seems to have a gentler spirit and prefers the sanctity of art and writing indoors to being out in the weather."

"And Queen Adeliza's health has improved enough to teach Emme skills with fabric."

"Then I am most blessed to have all of you here with me in this peaceful place."

✥ ✥ ✥

Past the gloaming, Adelaide reached for me. I cleared my throat to remove the lump.

"I have taken the Knights Templar vow of chastity, my love," I said with sadness.

Her wandering hand stopped at my words. She pulled away, smiled and nodded. "'Tis as it should be." She walked towards the door. "We are not wed and should never have—"

"Leave the past in the past, Adelaide."

She stared at me and then shrugged and curtsied. "It follows that I should leave you then. Can you *at least* sup with us?" Her tone was not lost on me.

"I . . . I can. I *will*," I managed with hesitancy. How I wanted to reach out to her and take her in my arms to love her physically as my heart loved her. She nodded and disappeared around the door, leaving behind a chill that found its way swiftly to my heart.

✥ ✥ ✥

We dined on an elegant meal of roasted boar and freshly-roasted vegetables from Adelaide's own garden. She and I stayed silent. I watched the children, sometimes catching myself staring at them in awe. How quickly they grew! Our dessert was a delectable pastry filled with fresh cream and a cup of sweet wine.

"No food has ever been better," I said. Leaning back in my chair I tried to meet Adelaide's eyes. She denied me. "I suppose now I need exercise."

I jumped up and popped Henry, Geoffrey, William, and Emme as I passed their heads. They hopped up and chased me all around the dining hall, all of us—even Adelaide and the dowager—giggling.

Henry stopped first. "I am old for such play."

"Nonsense! You should never grow too old for play," I called out to him. Still, he sat down and his brothers followed his lead. I swooped up Emme in my arms and spun her around as she giggled more. She was a beauty, like her mother. I kissed her rosy cheek and set her feet on the floor.

A nursemaid appeared to take them to their chambers for the night.

"Henry," I called out to my oldest son, "let us hunt on the morrow."

His face lit up. "Aye, Father! I have a new weapon to try."

"I will see you at dawn's first light then." He nodded and left behind the others while I joined the ladies at the table.

"He is delighted to have you home again. Even though Count Leofrick is marvelous with him, he is not their father. They . . . *we* . . . all need you," Adelaide emphasized.

Dowager Queen Adeliza cleared her throat. "We have all missed your presence, Sir Geoffrey. I hope your visits will become more frequent."

Visits.

The word made me shudder.

Have I become no more than a visitor in my own home?

She faked a yawn. "I am ready for bed. I will see you on the morrow. Rest well and have a good hunt with Henry." She walked a few steps before she glanced back. "Mayhap you will be surprised at his adeptness. Count Leofrick has taught him well."

"I owe Frick a great deal, it seems," I said. I lowered my head and bowed as the dowager left me alone with the most beautiful woman I had ever known. I gulped the rest of my wine and took her hand. She pulled back.

"Adelaide, we can still touch each other."

"I fear to do so," she whispered.

"For what cause?"

Her face turned to crimson. "I have longed for you so many nights, dreamed of you . . . us . . . in the throes of passion." Her face reddened. "I fear one touch would ignite wanting and I would not cause you to betray your vow."

I stared at her turned head and realized that to touch her would ignite a fire in me as well.

"I must find a way to be close to you and keep my vow. This is not fair to you, my beloved. Vows were meant for every man. Even those who are married have taken the vow."

"But, we are *not* married, Geoffrey, and never can we be. I should take Emme and leave this place so there is no more temptation for either of us to bear."

"No!" I shouted as she moved away. "No," I said more softly. "I will pray and meditate on this. An answer will come, my love."

She gave me a weak smile. "A room is prepared for you, Sir Geoffrey. Rest well; Henry's energy would be hard to handle for a lesser man."

"I will *not* sleep well, but I will rest nevertheless," I said grimly as I watched her move away from me.

✠ ✠ ✠

After a night of restless agitation, I walked down the long corridor at first light to my son, both of us dressed and carrying weapons to hunt 'til darkness forced us home. I nodded at my son, who held a sparkle in his eye I had never seen prior.

"To our mounts then," I announced.

We mounted up and trotted across the bridge to the pastures beyond, where the greyhounds were let loose. We moved at a slower gait behind the hounds, hoping to soon have hares within bow range and then in our pouches. Henry took the first hare at lightning speed with a perfect shot behind the ear.

"I see that you are worthy competition, my son," I said, smiling my approval.

"The game is on!" Henry left me behind on his swift steed but only for a moment. I rode up beside him and we let the horses loose.

Hunting with my son was exhilarating! By dusk we had killed three hares, a large stag and a wild boar with little said between us. As we headed back to the castle, Henry smiled at me.

"I wish to hunt with you more, Father," he said.

"I suppose you do, my son. You bested me at every turn."

We laughed and picked up our pace.

26

My trip to England began with a wind crossing the channel as chilled as the circumstance with Adelaide. Once on land again, I let Count gallop down paths through the forest afire with orange, red and yellow leaves. Some still clung to trees and many on the ground crunched under his hooves. I hoped I would not receive a frosty reception from King Stephen. My feelings towards him had softened over the years due, in part, to my maturity. But the undisputable fact was that his father—King Henry's brother—would have been king if death had not first claimed him. There had been rumors at the time that Henry played a role in his brother's death, thus making himself heir to the throne. I refused to believe it.

The sentry announced my arrival and even though Stephen welcomed me to his table at sunset, his demeanor held a distance, mayhap because of past controversy between us. I knelt before him.

"Welcome, Sir Geoffrey Plantagenet, Duke of Normandy. Please sit with me as my esteemed guest." He gestured to a fine seat behind the table board near him. I rose and joined him, a cup of wine set before me.

I sipped after watching him sip his cup first. "'Tis a fine wine."

"The vineyards surpassed themselves in many variations," the king said. He clapped his hands and servants appeared with bowls and trays of turnips, figs, apples and cheeses.

"Let us indulge until meat arrives."

I needed no prodding since all Count and I had eaten all day were wild berries along a ditch bank on our route. When roasted duck arrived, the king plated a healthy portion for himself and passed the tray to me. The meal ended with a bread pudding filled with apples and cinnamon, topped with a sweet cream.

"Join me in my private chamber, Sir Geoffrey." The king and I wiped our faces and hands.

"Your Grace," I said, nodding politely. We walked the familiar corridor of Windsor Castle that I had walked many times while in residence. A lump formed in my throat and kept me from uttering another word until we closed the door to his chamber. He dismissed his chamberlain and we seated ourselves near the hearth although no fire was present.

"You have travelled from Normandy *alone*, Sir Geoffrey," the king proclaimed. "Word arrived that you may now be called a Templar. I am impressed but not surprised." He reached for his throat. "I bear still the scar from your dagger's tip." He glared at me.

Composing an apology in my mind, it dissipated on my tongue when I looked into his eyes. I owed him nought.

He continued. "You came to the aid of a damsel in distress as a worthy and chivalrous knight should." I bowed my head in feigned respect. "But you humiliated me in front of all at Westminster. I have not forgotten," King Stephen declared.

"Nor have I. You and your men were guests of the king, yet you sprang on Queen Adeliza's lady to—"

"Ah, the lovely maiden. I do remember, but you stepped in to save her."

"Indeed."

The king lowered his head. "I merely toyed with her. Courtesans and fair maidens are at my beck and call. Fret not. I have no need of your maiden, Sir Geoffrey Plantagenet." He drank down a cup of wine and I continued to sip mine.

"Tell me then, Sir Geoffrey, what fetches you back to England?"

"You will not be surprised to learn the future of my first-born son and that of Matilda is my primary concern," I blurted.

"Ah, and how *is* the Lady of the English these days?" His tone owned an air of sarcasm I cared not for.

"I know not. We are apart but I will go to her after my visit with you, sire."

"I will relieve your mind, Sir Geoffrey," the king whispered as he leaned towards me. "I have a son, Eustace, who is heir-apparent. However, I still meet with those who are loyal to King Henry's memory. 'Tis shameful Matilda became such a shrew that she turned many of the royal court against her. She had won their favor, you know." He shifted in his velvet chair. "'Twas with ease I regained their support once her true nature revealed itself."

I nodded slightly. No words seemed needed. I could not defend Matilda's actions.

"Even though my father, the rightful heir to the English throne, died under suspicious circumstances, my uncle Henry took advantage. I cannot fault him for that, but *I* was rightful heir upon *his* death. When King Henry died with you and your lady wife in another country, I offered decisive leadership at a moment when England and Normandy teetered on the brink of chaos. I had not anticipated civil war . . . years of it . . . to exhaust me so."

"Indeed, Your Grace."

"The monarchy belongs to male, not female."

I bobbed my head in his direction. "Matilda and I knew a battle for the throne would ensue. I blame you not for wielding your military power with the aid of those loyal to your plight. But young Henry is a scholar and learns all matters of government from his mother. He is a soldier who strengthens with each day."

He disregarded my statement.

"In another time we might have been allies, Sir Geoffrey." Another awkward silence filled the chamber, and when I did not respond, he sighed deeply. "Alas, Eustace is the rightful heir."

"Your Grace, I am here to ask that the royal heir, young Henry, succeed you. He is adept at reading, writing, several languages, and mathematics. He is an archer and now competing in jousting tournaments." I cleared my throat before continuing. "Your son, Eustace, has a reputation of plundering and raping. He—"

"I have no cause to place your Henry on the throne and ignore my *own* son, Sir Geoffrey," the king interrupted with anger in his voice. "I will speak no more of this!"

With a heavy heart, I rose to leave.

"I have met your son, Sir Geoffrey. He *is* impressive and determined. I will not forget him," the king said.

I bowed and left with no further mention of my son's earlier impulsive visit, and with little hope that I had planted a seed in Stephen's mind.

✤ ✤ ✤

Even though thick rain accompanied me back across the channel to the priory at Notre Dame, I let Count travel at his own pace until rain fell so heavily I pulled the reins and coaxed him into a dense forest for shelter. I dismounted and tied him to a low limb and wandered around to find a place to relieve myself of all I had eaten at the palace. I sat under a low limb near my mount and fell asleep, hypnotized by the rain's steady cadence. I was startled awake by his whinny and stared into the eyes of a curious deer. When I jumped, she jumped and ran towards deeper woods. I adjusted myself and saw rain had ceased. Sun dried my garments as I rode on to the priory.

Once I arrived I waited in an outer room to be announced.

"Lady Matilda will see you now, Sir Geoffrey Plantagenet, Duke of Normandy." I followed the nun to a tall oak door inside the stone building and tapped.

"Enter," I heard a soft voice call out.

"Lady Matilda?"

"Geoffrey, come in," she answered. I found it hard to believe that soft reverent voice came from my shrew. "You look well, my husband."

"I am blessed."

"You grow more handsome with age." She walked across the small room away from me. Without turning, she asked, "How is Henry?"

"Tall and handsome. He is a scholar and an archer."

She turned in my direction, her face pale and drawn. "An archer? Then he will become a worthy knight."

"Indeed. And young Geoffrey is full of mischief enough to be adept as well." She spoke not. "And young William, alas, has no interest in military pursuits. He enjoys his readings and the arts."

She still said nought.

I cleared my throat. "Matilda, I have come to tell you I have met with King Stephen."

"Oh?"

"On our Henry's behalf. I wanted you to know the state of the matter."

She turned and faced me, her eyes meeting mine. "And in what state *is* the matter?"

I cleared my throat. "Negotiations were unfavorable, I fear. He plans to leave the throne to his despicable son, Eustace." I waited for a response but none came. "The royal court of nobles once opened the Westminster gates for you, Matilda." I pointed my accusing finger in her direction.

"Remind me *not* of my malicious superiority. I serve my penance here," she declared, lowering her head. "My cousin's decision surprises me not. And Eustace, I hear, is the devil's spawn."

"I feared as much. But I am pleased to announce I will name our son, Henry, the Duke of Normandy, due to my oath as a Templar."

"But Henry is young, my husband."

"I will appoint Count Leofrick to oversee and protect Henry, Geoffrey and William when I am abroad," I explained. "You, my lady wife, should assist Henry in learning more about the administration of government and how to become a military power to be reckoned with."

"The squire pulled from muck is now a *count*? He will protect my sons?"

"He is indeed a fine count. Our family is in good hands."

"And how is Dowager Queen Adeliza?"

"She thrives with the love of the children."

"I send her best regards," Matilda spoke, looking me in the eye. "I will prepare Henry for his rightful place on the throne of England, my husband," she said with determination.

I nodded and left, heading back to Adelaide and the children.

27

My contented reunion back in Anjou was short-lived. The breathless messenger entered the gate and dismounted noisily. I recognized him and his demeanor and ran to him.

"Sir Geoffrey, your father . . ."

"What is amiss, Dafyd?"

"Your father Fulk V, King of Jerusalem, is killed."

"No!" I shouted in disbelief. "Murdered by that treacherous infidel?"

"No, my lord. While on a hunting trip his horse stumbled and fell. King Fulk's skull was crushed under the saddle, sir," Dafyd spoke in a soft voice.

My heart hitched. "Where *is* my father?"

"He was carried back to the hunting lodge at Acre where he died, my lord. His body will be delivered back to Jerusalem."

I stared at the man and tried to wrap my head and heart around his words before patting his shoulders.

"Rest, Dafyd. We will refresh your mount and ride together to Jerusalem."

I noticed Frick was beside me with a somber face. "Pray peace continues here and all over the realm for I must return to Jerusalem to bury my father."

Frick and Henry prepared mounts and Adelaide food for my woeful journey. As we mounted, Queen Adeliza approached and touched my elbow.

"Queen Melisende adored the man behind the title, Geoffrey. I send deepest sympathy." She stepped back and Adelaide handed me the food parcel.

"I trust this will be enough for the long travel," she said, looking up at me with sad eyes.

"It will do," I answered with a smile. "I leave you again, my love, but I will return to you."

"Your blessed homecoming will be anticipated."

Frick wished to accompany me, but I needed him in Normandy to assure our hinterlands did not take advantage of our vulnerable circumstances.

❖ ❖ ❖

My father was buried in the Church of the Holy Sepulcher with royalty from many countries in attendance and an army of Templar Knights dressed in full mantle. I positioned myself beside Queen Melisende and her son, Baldwin III, heir-apparent at thirteen summers and my father's son during the long and elaborate farewell. I had seen the young heir twice in all the years my father was married to Melisende, and although he was my half-brother, I knew little of him. He displayed at all times a healthy distrust of my presence at my own father's funeral. I turned my attention back to the requiem for my father but glanced at Baldwin occasionally.

Everard des Barres walked to the podium first and began my father's history as a tribute.

"Baldwin II, King of Jerusalem, who fathered no son of his own, sent a delegation to France, requesting that Louis VII select from French nobility a man suitable to marry the beautiful Melisende, his daughter. Fulk V, then Count of Anjou, was the king's choice. He had been on a pilgrimage here to Jerusalem and was a faithful, gentle and affable kind, a great ruler of his own people, an experienced warrior and wise in all military affairs. He was a loving husband to Melisende." She nodded. "And a good father to his sons." Baldwin III bowed his head and then cut his eyes in my direction. Did he for some reason see me as a threat? I was nought to him.

I nodded as Everard met my eyes. Tributes continued on while I lost myself in memories coupled with melancholy.

Once the celebration of my father's life ended, I mounted up for the long journey back to Normandy. I sped back home, where Henry was knighted at the northern post of Carlisle by King David, who had taken to the young lad in spite of his mother. Then we traveled back to Rouen where I handed over the governing of the duchy to my son with great pride.

Once I named young Henry Duke of Normandy, Eustace—recently knighted himself—attacked Normandy, but my young son valiantly led his army against the king's son and defeated him with dispatch. I had no doubt his father knew nought of this attack, but Stephen, in the seventeenth summer of his reign, tried to have Eustace crowned. However, the king's brother, Theobald, Archbishop of Canterbury, fled the country rather than crown a usurper's son who had made threats against bishops and blatantly demanded contributions from religious houses all over England. Eustace, long known for an arrogance that made him many enemies, was killed soon thereafter— some say struck down "by God's wrath" while he plundered church lands near Bury St. Edmunds.

The death of Eustace presented the opportunity to speak to Stephen once again. I met with Matilda and we arranged to travel together to give our condolences to King

Stephen. After all, they were first cousins and Stephen had been her father's favorite nephew.

We had an amicable trip across the channel. As we landed on English soil, lightning warned us to seek shelter. We dined and overnighted at an inn in Canterbury, where we were welcomed at the tavern and enjoyed ale and tall tales from other travelers. Trovers entertained us with story- telling, singing the story while they played a strange musical instrument we had never before seen or heard. They sang of love, politics and laments. Even though the inn was dank and dark, I studied Matilda in the torch light. Her demeanor had altered and she seemed happier and more carefree—at peace—and still a beautiful woman.

We waited out the storm that dumped enough rain to overflow streams, brooks, and rivers. Once rainfall ended and the sun appeared, we made our way through mud and sludge to Westminster and stopped at the gate to be announced. When we were allowed to enter King Stephen's private chamber, I was shocked at how much the man had failed in appearance and vitality since my last visit. Matilda curtsied and I bowed.

"Your Grace, we have come far to extend our condolences. We cannot imagine your pain on the loss of a son," I said.

He lifted eyes filled with sorrow and motioned us to a huge wooden table. He sat on the end and gestured Matilda to his right and me to his left.

"Sir Geoffrey, would you be kind enough to fetch wine and pour us all a cup?"

I bowed again, walked to the sideboard and picked up two decanters. A servant handed me a board with warm manchets and a wedge of cheese to carry back to the table. I poured in silence, glancing at my lady wife, also silent.

"Ah, this fine wine does take the edge off," Stephen said, guzzling his drink and pouring himself more from the decanter nearest him. He stared at Matilda until her cheeks reddened and she smiled and bowed her head modestly.

"You are still a beauty, my cousin Matilda. You made a worthy opponent on the battlefield. You have earned my respect, but I am exhausted from battles and wars, and now with the death of Eustace, my son and heir apparent, I find the very wind knocked from my lungs. My heart is heavy."

I walked over and sat near my lady wife. "What of your other son?"

"He went into the monastery years ago, Sir Geoffrey. He has no desire to rule a nation of any size. He witnessed power bringing with it wars of control that distressed him. Eustace was strong physically and relished conflict. But alas, he is no more."

"I have no wish to fight you further for land or title, King Stephen. We are here to ask if we can do anything to ease your heart's pain," Matilda said with ease and a soft voice. I almost believed her words myself although I knew better.

The king stood. "Let us walk in the garden." We followed him through a side door and into a courtyard filled with plants and flowers of great beauty.

"The orchids are divine," Matilda said as she stopped just short of touching one of the delicate blooms she cared nought about.

"My queen busied herself here." He paused. "She did until the news arrived. Now she stays cloistered in her chamber and under covers. Her heart is broken as well." He walked on. "I have been punished for outwitting others, especially you, Matilda. I took advantage of you at your lowest point, but I still believe the throne was rightfully mine. My father, had he lived, would have been king rather than his younger brother, my Uncle Henry."

Matilda bit her lower lip but did not speak, although I know not how she kept quiet.

Stephen turned to face both of us. "I know you are not here merely to extend condolences." We glanced at each other. "Your Henry is what . . . eighteen summers now?"

"Soon nineteen, Your Grace," I answered.

"I have met him, you know. He is an impressive lad, indeed."

"We know of his rambunctious attempt, King Stephen, and I took no part in it," Matilda hastened to say. "Henry's foolish escapade did nought to please us. He is at times hotheaded," Matilda announced, looking at me, "like his father."

"*And* his mother, my cousin," Stephen added. "You would have been much more prepared financially and with sturdy warriors rather than young misfits."

The king threw back his head and laughed. "He came to me not with arrogance but with humility, and requested pay for his motley train—my would-be attackers." He shook his head. "Presumptuous, indeed. I paid and sent him away."

"Henry was headstrong and presumptuous on that occasion, but he learned a lesson and shows remorse," Matilda added, shaking her head. "I can assure you we knew nought of this until he returned home with his backside between his spurs."

The king emitted a slow but sad chuckle and nodded his head. "Your lad has a magnetic personality. He walked in with boldness but with respect to title if not to the man. I could not resist testing him. Young Henry is driven and ambitious, and I have no doubt he will return to unseat me some time in the future. He is intelligent, with the fire of his grandfather, his namesake, Matilda. You know how close your father and I were." He leaned towards her.

She nodded and we watched the king drift somewhere we could not follow. Perchance a melancholy into which we were not invited. We stayed quiet and watched him for any signs of awareness. Unexpectedly he jerked himself upright and looked at both of us.

"Then 'tis settled," Stephen declared. "I will make my wishes known to nobles and clergy that upon my death, your Henry will become King of England." Stephen stood. "We have made our peace at last. Have an unhindered journey home."

We had been abruptly dismissed, so we bowed and walked away. After we passed through the gate Matilda reached over to squeeze my hand.

✤ ✤ ✤

I was told Stephen was immediately unnerved by a lack of defense against a new and charismatic Duke of Normandy, his revered grandfather's namesake and every inch his rightful heir.

Both Matilda and I set about gaining allegiance with the church and divided magnates in hopes our Henry would be crowned Henry II at some future time.

28

When I arrived back at Loches Castle, I embraced Adelaide with every fiber of my being, elated the tide had turned in Henry's direction and I could spend time in my own domain with my family rather than afar battling foes.

After greeting the children and the dowager queen after darkness had set in, Adelaide and I were alone in the long dark corridor. I reached for her. I first stroked her long luminous hair then dared to touch her neck, moving my fingers to her soft rosy cheeks.

"Dare not!" She pushed me and walked away.

"I must, my love," I confessed in an agonized whisper that stopped her walk.

"Your vows, Geoffrey," she said, facing me but taking a step farther away from my touch.

"The sight of you even from afar tempts me beyond measure. I try to resist, but God help me, I cannot. I yield to your exquisite beauty and our undeniable devotion one to the other. I hope my God can forgive me. Surely he understands this is no tryst but true love."

"Oh, Geoffrey," she whispered.

I took the steps needed to reach her and folded her into my hungry arms, my desire evident against her body as it melted into mine. We rushed through my chamber door and disappeared behind it to let long pent-up desire loose.

✤ ✤ ✤

Three winters came and went as Adelaide and I enjoyed each other and watched the children grow. Peace reigned in this place, if not in my own heart, filled with guilt for not upholding my vow of chastity. I prayed daily that God would forgive me. Adelaide and I remained discreetly in separate chambers and hoped others would not become wise to our recurrent retreats behind locked doors or rides into the country to be alone. I had no desire to ruin Adelaide's reputation or show due cause to be removed from the Templar order because I loved this woman. In my heart I could not believe that loving her physically could displease God, but man—Hugues of Payen—might not have so forgiving a nature.

Henry, more polished and experienced in all matters of government, had grown taller and stronger. Muscle defined his torso from practicing archery and jousting on a daily basis. His riding skills improved with each ride outside the gates and his own rides to study at his mother's side at the priory. Young Geoffrey, even though small in size, had calmed into a pleasant young man enamored with wood and gem stones. Frick taught him to build saddles and my recent gift was one bejeweled for elaborate show. William, by far the quietest child, entertained himself with reading and painting landscapes. Emme wove rich and colorful tapestries to hang all over the castle walls. Queen Adeliza had sent all over the continent for exquisite dyes that made Emme and William beam with pleasure.

One mid-day I sat beside my mistress and held her hand. "My dear Adelaide, Edessa has been besieged in a border war. Queen Melisende sent an army, but to no avail. Edessa fell to Zengi, an evil Seljuk Turk and may well mark the beginning of fierce Muslim reaction to the Crusades. Baldwin III's small army of troops then attacked. Jerusalem and Damascus have long been on good terms because of my father's efforts. 'Tis no longer true. My half-brother is a young and inexperienced king, having shared the crown with his mother until he reached age. Now he wars with her and with the Zengi. He cannot win without reinforcements. Pope Eugene III calls for another Crusade along with King Louis of France. As a Knight Templar, I must see to my duty to defend the Holy Land."

"Is there no peace treaty?"

"'Tis no more. And with no treaty, Damascus will never trust Crusader states again. The loss of a sympathetic Muslim state will, I fear, cause much sorrow far into the future." I gathered her into my arms and kissed her forehead. "Baldwin undoes all good peace my father made," I added with sorrow.

"Do not leave again, Geoffrey, I beg you."

"I made a vow."

"You too made a marked vow of chastity." Her tone was harsh.

"Adelaide!" I bellowed her name in anger and watched her cower in the corner. I bit my lower lip and remained quiet until my anger turned to sadness and I went to her.

"My beloved, I must go," I spoke in a whisper.

"But Geoffrey, 'tis a far journey and not of our land. Your absence spans much time. Why must you go?"

"During the First Crusade the Kingdom of Jerusalem, Antioch, and the county of Edessa ruled as Crusader states. As I have told you, Edessa is small and underpopulated, thus its weak state subjects it to frequent attacks from Muslim states. The Crusader states never have ample fighting men. When my father died, Zengi besieged Edessa, taking full advantage of the situation. The King of Jerusalem, the prince of Antioch and the counts of Edessa and Tripoli cannot between them raise more than a thousand knights.

"Baldwin was foolish to attack Damascus. He has now aligned himself with the Byzantine Empire. The situation is tense between the remaining Crusader states. Tripoli and Antioch assert their independence but have not the army to defend themselves against this Turkish tyrant. Zengi will no doubt continue to take control of weakness, including Damascus, unless the Templars intervene."

As tears soaked her cheeks, she touched my face with her silky hand. "You take my heart with you, Geoffrey Plantagenet."

"And I leave my heart here with you." Lowering my head, I placed a tender kiss on her soft lips and left the arms of my love. I walked swiftly to the younger children and kissed each one before I moved around the castle to give Frick the news.

"Will we travel to Jerusalem then?"

"We are summoned to The Temple Mount in the city of David. I know not what awaits us, Frick. As much as I want you there beside me, I pray you will relieve my mind of worry on *this* front. An unknown squire will be appointed for me there."

His face fell in disappointment but his recovery was swift.

"I honor you by protecting them and the new Duke of Normandy and future King of England, Sir Geoffrey."

"Teach Henry all you know, Frick. Lady Matilda sees to his knowledge of politics and government. He needs great knowledge on all matters. He is young still, and your guidance is paramount while I am abroad." I patted his shoulders. "Tell him not of my journey. I fear he might follow and he is ill-prepared."

"Aye, m'lord."

I headed to the stable where my Arabians were saddled. "Godspeed, m'lord," he called behind me.

✤ ✤ ✤

My men and I had no sooner left the duchy than the sky darkened and wind howled, turning the day's warmth into cold. At our first rest, we layered more clothing and draped our mounts in Templar cuirass.

"Let us hasten while the wind is at our backs," I directed. We rode with speed until near the gloaming, pitched tents in a meadow surrounded by forest, and banked a fire to sleep near.

"On the morrow we cross into treacherous mountains made all the more so by winter's fury." We all studied a starless sky and prayed our journey would not stall.

At first light, I peeked out of my tent flap at hoar frost on the ground.

"Frost opens the gate for snow. We need to hasten," I said.

"I will prepare the horses," Hardouin muttered.

"I will set a board for food," Blou stated.

"Leave the board. We will eat on the move," I called to him.

We dismantled tents and stored them on our mounts. "We should reach the mountains by noontide and cross Brenner Pass—the lowest and easiest of the Alps—if the weather holds."

With rested mounts and enough food to sustain us, we traveled with speed through the valley between two ragged forests until land grew into hills and then mountains that slowed us to a crawl. I looked up foothills at snow already fallen and frozen there. Bundling up, we ascended winding highlands and let our horses find the safest path. Our mounts struggled up crags past stiff and twisted brush, their heads down, looking for the safest placement of hooves. I held on tightly as Honor's powerful body took me upward to the pinnacle.

"Ahead of us the terrain is a greater challenge. Let us stay one behind the other as we cross the pass," Hardouin advised.

On the morrow I looked out at sun's rays coming down through trees with snow-covered branches on a frigid morning. Mounting up, I patted Honor's face and we started the difficult rise as the day darkened. Dampness in the air crept into my bones and I wrapped my wool cloak tighter and encouraged my mount to creep on up and over the acme so our journey down the mountain could relieve us all. We reached the summit and started a downward trek when Honor stumbled and flipped me from my saddle, rock rushing to meet my face and head. I pulled myself up and managed to hold on to Honor's reins.

"Geoffrey, you are hurt!"

"Fret not, Blou. I am whole."

"Your face bleeds," he pointed out. I wiped blood from my nose and felt how tender my face had become. The rock scored a victory against it and behind my right ear.

"Mayhap I should wear my helmet to protect myself from the dastardly rock," I said to ease tension. I managed a weak laugh and rubbed the back of my head. They joined in with their own attempt at laughter before we led our mounts cautiously down to a flat ridge where we rested for the night, our camp set among the rocks. While we slept in stillness, cold dampness came down with darkness. Snow blanketed all paths that led down and away from the treacherous Alps.

"I fear we must wait out the weather," Hardouin declared.

"We are needed in Jerusalem! We are expected. And we have yet to deal with the hostility ahead," I argued.

"Once the weather breaks, we can travel the Christian lands of Constantinople but, alas, the hostiles of Asia Minor will cut us to pieces dare we not prepare for them. We must avoid Turks or take our last breaths in their land," Blou added.

"This will make for longer travel."

"'Tis our lot, Sir Geoffrey," the wise Hardouin said. My head throbbed with pain and emotion.

"The path is mired and impassable, Geoffrey." His older eyes bored into mine. "Far better to arrive at all than have our bones found crushed at the bottom of this ridge. Mayhap we can devise a plan to skirt the Turks while we wait." Hardouin studied the surroundings more closely.

Entrapped in our tent, we slept, told stories and ventured out to track small animals in the daylight, among them pheasant we flushed and chased to eat with bread cakes. During one cold dark night, isolated from the rest of mankind in the snowy Alps, I sat up and whispered to both of them.

"My blood boils to begin battle, but I must confess when I remember faces of my childhood dead on the field of battle, I fight with reluctance. I am forever tarnished by that carnage."

"We slew many," Hardouin admitted with a nod.

"The weak and ill-prepared," I added.

"'Tis war, Geoffrey." Hardouin stepped towards me. "Preparation is key when the enemy is near."

"The battle in the Holy Land is not the same, Geoffrey." Blou grabbed my shoulders. "We are now fighting the infidels. Remember that and you will strike with deadly force."

Hardouin nodded in agreement. Blou's words struck me and I nodded as well.

✤ ✤ ✤

As tight quarters began to close in on us and flatulence from beans became a contest, a break in the weather kept us from turning on each other.

"The sun warms the earth. I will enlist my spade on soft snow and mayhap reveal a path where we can begin our descent," Blou said. Hardouin and I broke camp and picked dried berries that dangled from a bush I had shaken.

Travel was slow but we reached flatter land by dark and rested for a full-out gallop on the morrow. We made good time then, and crossed the peninsula between the Black Sea and the Mediterranean Sea. We reached the border near the county of Edessa where recent battle had wreaked havoc on the land. We watered our mounts and rested as troop after troop of Templar knights, headed not towards Edessa, but back towards Antioch.

"I fear we have arrived after the battle," Hardouin stated.

I approached a knight who had dismounted for water. He looked over at me.

"King Baldwin III was no match for Zengi. The battle was brief but brutal," he told me.

"And what of my half-brother, Baldwin III?"

"Your half-brother, aye? He lives yet his mount cut from beneath him. He and his small army limped away to lick their wounds."

Though our disappointment in finding no battle ruled the day, we joined others and rode at a slow pace through the principality of Antioch on past many castles and into the county of Tripoli. Some knights detoured into Damascus, others left behind at the Sea of Galilee. Our arduous trek across the continent would not end until we arrived in Jerusalem at the temple on Mount Moriah—

known as the Temple Mount—where Templars would gather. Tired, hungry, and forlorn, we partook of barrels of wine before fatigue sent us to bed down, our mounts in the stables beyond.

❖ ❖ ❖

Over the rest of winter and far into summer we protected pilgrims from Jaffa to Jerusalem from bandits and Turkish rogues. Zengi controlled Edessa. We hoped our presence would keep him from gaining more lands. We patrolled the kingdom, on the lookout for rogues or armies. With little rain, the earth dried and cracked open, begging for moisture to keep it in place. My head and heart ached to return to Normandy.

Hugues of Payen assigned his most-trusted men—I among them—another task as well. We excavated and mined tunnels under our quarters on the Temple Mount. The Temple Mount was believed to be above the ruins of the Temple of Solomon where holy relics had been hidden or buried. Our charge was to find sacred treasures from the time of Christ and present them to Hugues who wished to take artifacts back to Europe along with an envoy of Templars to guard them.

29

"Hold!" I shouted into the dusty air, brushing clay and stone fragments away from a stone wall as other knights stalled behind and beside me. We gently pulled on treasure to free it from its hiding place in a large crevice in the rock. Men dusted it off as I stood back to catch my breath.

"'Mayhap 'tis Pipe rolls," Edmund of Cyprus said. He studied the bundles. Another knight moved closer for a look.

"Mayhap scriptural scrolls." He unrolled one and then another. "They appear to be treatises on sacred geometry," he called out to all curious knights.

"I have heard ancient wisdom is buried here," Thomas of Antioch said. "Let us find more."

"Let us *rest*," we heard a familiar voice say from the tunnel. Hugues smiled. "Your diligence is in need of reward. Let us celebrate this discovery with baths and a feast."

With great relief, we left the dark, dank and dust-laden tunnel for our reward. My bath was much-needed, and I savored it even though many knights splashed and played near me. I had no interest in joining in their antics. I left the bath, dressed and walked into the temple to be alone. I had been surrounded by boisterous men for as long as I could endure and now wanted and needed meditation.

As I knelt, quieted and prayed, I felt the mighty presence of God all around me and savored the sensation much more than I had savored the bath. I prayed more, asking God to protect and care for my family back home, the family I could not seem to return to soon enough. I also pleaded with God to forgive me my sins.

"I am blemished, my Lord, and seek your everlasting forgiveness from all my sins," I whispered in earnest, tears pouring down my face. My shoulders began to tremble.

As I stayed quiet, I felt gracious and merciful peace wash over me for the first time in my life.

30

After more months of seeking sacred treasure, we began our journey north and approached arid and barren lands near Damascus in a high wind, looking over mountaintops with great concern. The sky turned from clear blue to cloudy to brown and rusted red. I smelled it even before I felt it. The dust storm befell us across war-ravaged earth more rapidly than we could take cover. Caught far away from shelter, we dismounted and grabbed what we could from our packs to cover our horses and ourselves.

I unfurled my canvas tent and threw it over Honor and myself, peering out to see if I needed to share with another warrior. I searched for Paeri and saw his struggle to cover many mounts at the back of our train. As I stepped towards him with Honor, the storm plowed into me and knocked me off my feet like a sack of grain, holding me face down in the dirt. Honor sank to the ground beside me to await the storm's completion.

The dense dust sped over our train, pinned us to the ground and pelted my back through the canvas. I tried to save my breath for as long as I could. I knew the dust could suffocate me if given the chance. I covered my face as much as I could while still holding canvas around us. Fortunately Honor lay on part of the canvas and kept it from soaring away never to be seen again. The storm did not relent until I was almost out of short puffs of air.

Once I heard coughing and voices elsewhere, I peeked out to see the enormous cloud of dust had passed us and bore down on small villages between us and Israel. Mayhap people there had seen its approach and had more time to prepare than we had close to the mountains. John of Izmir dusted himself off and ran to untangle men from their canvases. Honor rose and I put away my tent. I made certain my men were out of harm's way and in satisfactory condition. We gathered our packs and mounts. With a fresh wind at our backs, we pushed onward.

❖ ❖ ❖

We made the long arduous journey to France with Hugues of Payen leading us. I looked forward to a reunion with my family who would meet me there. Days later our train stopped at the end of a meadow and we watered our mounts in the River Loir and there cleansed ourselves. Although the cold water refreshed, my body felt odd and the unrelenting pain in my head staggered me. I did not linger long in the water. Geese disturbed by our presence swam away and honked discontent back at us.

The bright day made the view of the castle's spire appear closer than I knew it to be, but we continued to move towards our destination. The Templar Grand Master had made short hair and beards mandatory, so I arrived at Chateau-du-Loir unrecognizable to my children behind a thick long beard the color of persimmon that seemed to have fallen away from my head and grown on my chin. I dismounted and held on to Honor for stability as I turned to face my family.

"I would know those eyes anywhere," Adelaide called out. "'Tis your father, Sir Geoffrey Plantagenet, arrived at last!"

I gave her a feeble smile and coughed.

She ran to me. "Geoffrey, you shiver." She touched my wet face. "You are ill."

"I need nought but rest, my love, and you beside me," I replied. I wiped sweat from my face to hold her close, to smell her, to see those channel eyes again.

"We tried herbs, but alas, they did no good," Hardouin whispered to her.

Once inside the castle, I stumbled, not able to keep my feet in a straight path to my assigned chamber.

Adelaide grabbed me and shouted over her shoulder. "Find the physician! Make haste!"

Leofrick, who had brought my family to me, grabbed my arm on the other side and together they led me to a bed where I collapsed atop its covers.

My weakness continued and brought to mind the crone's words: "Heat of Broom becomes your doom." People scurried around me but I knew only Leofrick and Adelaide.

"He is fevered," I heard the physician tell Adelaide as I sweated and shivered. My body seemed unwilling to stop its onslaught and my head throbbed in a constant rhythm. She mopped my face with cool water, concern written on her brow.

"I must tell you, Geoffrey, King Stephen is dead and your Henry will at last become king. Do you hear me, Geoffrey? All of your sacrifices have been worthwhile," she told me.

I attempted a satisfied smile but knew I would not see my son ascend the throne. Tears dampened my eyes as I spoke my final wishes for my heirs and lands to Robert of Semblancay, who wrote my will.

Later in the day, voices took on a reverberation that moved farther and farther away from where I lay, but I knew Adelaide stayed close and held my hand, Frick not far behind her. Faces distorted—even that of Adelaide—as I struggled to identify them. I continued to shake under heavy wool as the day's last light dimmed. Shadows grew long and the final candlelight sputtered and plunged me into eternal nightfall.

EPILOGUE

The popular young Henry ascended the throne of England, becoming King Henry II. He was a worthy king who brought war-devastated England a new age of peace. But the Plantagenets had no trust for one another, and by the end of the fifteenth century, a staggering number of kings and royal dukes had been murdered, executed, or died in battle.

During this epic period known as The War of the Roses, a vicious family feud developed between two branches of the Plantagenet royal dynasty, descended through different sons of King Edward III. The House of York was represented by the white rose, The House of Lancaster by the red. The fight was on to rule the island kingdom of England.

The Yorkist king Richard III, the last of his house, was killed at Bosworth Field. The male line of the Plantagenets became extinct with the execution of Edward, Earl of Warwick, the son of George, Duke of Clarence in the reign of Henry VII, the first Tudor.

Dear Reader,

Would you consider writing a review on Amazon.com? Your review doesn't have to be lengthy or complicated but would be appreciated.

Thank you.

About the Author

Award-winning multi-genre author Susan Whitfield is a native of North Carolina. She is the author of five published mysteries, *Genesis Beach*, *Just North of Luck*, *Hell Swamp*, *Sin Creek* and *Sticking Point*, all set in the state she loves.

She also authored *Killer Recipes*, a unique cookbook that includes recipes from mystery writers around the country. All proceeds from this book are donated to cancer research.

Slightly Cracked is her first women's fiction, set in Wayne County where she lives with her husband. Their two sons live nearby with their families.

Sprig of Broom is her first historical fiction about a medieval ancestor and is set in twelfth century England and Normandy.

Susan's books are available in print and all e-book formats.